ART SKILLS LAB

COMIC BOOK SKILLS LAB

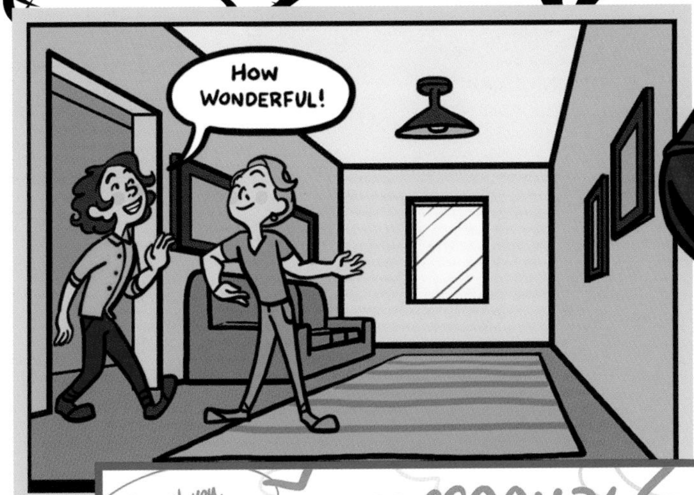
How WONDERFUL!

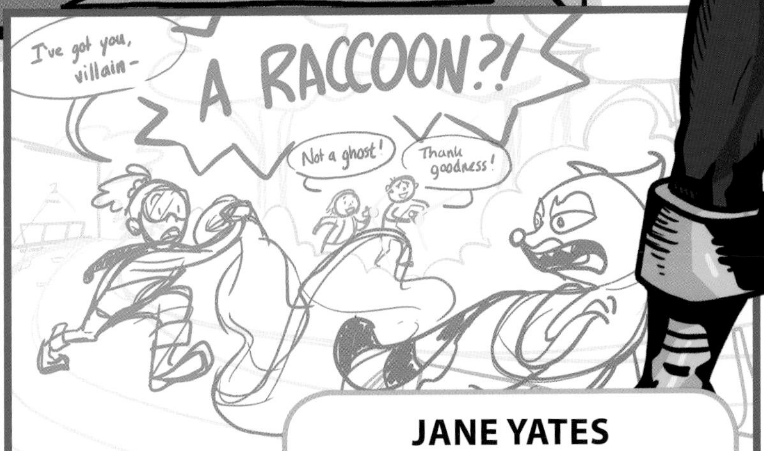
I've got you, villain-
A RACCOON?!
Not a ghost!
Thank goodness!

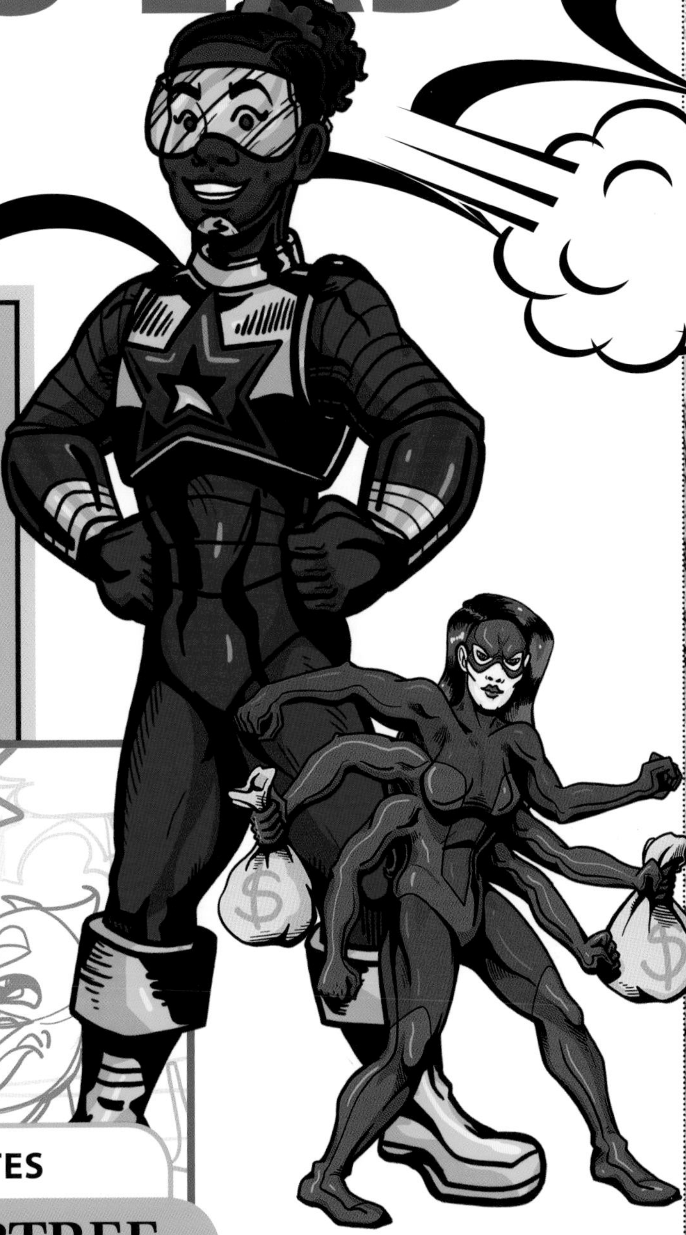

JANE YATES

CRABTREE
PUBLISHING COMPANY
WWW.CRABTREEBOOKS.COM

ART SKILLS LAB

Author
Jane Yates

Editors
Marcia Abramson,
Kathy Middleton

Photo research
Melissa McClellan

Cover/Interior Design
T.J. Choleva

Proofreader
Crystal Sikkens

**Production coordinator
and Prepress technician**
Tammy McGarr

Print coordinator
Katherine Berti

Developed and produced for
Crabtree Publishing by
BlueApple*Works* Inc.

Consultant
Trevor Hodgson
Fine artist and former director of The Dundas
Valley School of Art

Art & Photographs
Shutterstock.com: © jirawat phueksriphan
(cover top); © Prostock-studio (cover bottom
left); © TinyDoz (cover type); © Sarawut
Aiemsinsuk (cover middle left); © FabrikaSimf
(cover middle right); © Excellent backgrounds
(background); © Ruslan Huzau (p. 4 left);
MemoAngeles (p. 11 top left); humphrey(p. 11
top right);FrameAngel (p. 5 right middle); ©
KOKTARO (p. 5 bottom left); © ETIENjones
(p. 6 top left); © IPOP (p. 6 top middle); ©
Piyato (p. 6 middle left); © Be Good (p. 6
middle, middle); © ajt (p. 6 middle right); ©
chrisatpps (p. 6 bottom left); © Tabuda Y (p. 7
middle left);

Instructive illustrations © Fiona Wadsley
cover, p. 6– 29 unless otherwise noted

Public Domain: Harrison Cady((p. 4 right),
Image provided by: Library of Congress,
Washington, DC; Jack Binder/Fawcett Comics
(p. 5 top left); Louis Zansky (pencil) and Fred
Eng (inks) (p. 5 left second from top); Maurice
Whitman (p. 5 left second from bottom); Frank
Frazetta (p. 5 bottom left); Will Eisner (pencils)
and Lou Fine (inks) (p. 5 bottom right); Victor

E. Pazmiño (p. 10, 11 bottom right); Ralph
Mayo (p. 11 middle left); Ken Battefield (p.
11 bottom left); Rudolph Dirks (p. 13 bottom
right); Jimmy Frise (p. 17 bottom left); C. C.
Beck (p. 21 bottom; p. 22 bottom); Will Eisner
(p. 23 bottom); Alex Schomburg (p. 25 bottom)

GOLDEN ERA COMICS LIST -
(p. 5 top left, top to bottom): Wow comic
number 38, 1941; Classics Comics book,
Robin Hood, Dec 1942; Planet Comics, issue
71, Fiction House, 1953; Beware number 10,
July 1954; (p. 5 bottom right): Wonderworld
Comics number 3, 1939; (p. 10): The Black
Terror #11, Page 32 August, 1945; (p. 11):
America's Best Comics #22, Page 17, June,
1947; (p. 11 bottom left): America's Best
Comics #22, Page 25, June, 1947; (p. 11 bottom
right): The Black Terror #11, Page 31 August,
1945; (p. 21 bottom left):Whiz Comics number
22, October, 1941; (p. 21 bottom right): Captain
Marvel Adventures number 17, November
1942; (p. 21 top right): Whiz Comics number 2,
February 1940; (p. 22): America's Best Comics
#20, page 39 December 1946; (p. 23 bottom
top): The Spirit, 11 March 1951; (p. 23 bottom
left):The Spirit, number 18, November 1949;
(p. 23 bottom right): The Spirit, number 21,
June 1950; (p. 25 bottom left): Speed Comics,
number 34, September 1944; (p. 25 top right):
Speed Comics, number 32, May 1944

Library and Archives Canada Cataloguing in Publication

Title: Comic book skills lab / Jane Yates.
Names: Yates, Jane, author.
Series: Art skills lab.
Description: Series statement: Art skills lab | Includes index.
Identifiers: Canadiana (print) 20200151517 |
  Canadiana (ebook) 20200151525 |
  ISBN 9780778768432 (hardcover) |
  ISBN 9780778768470 (softcover) |
  ISBN 9781427124296 (HTML)
Subjects: LCSH: Comic books, strips, etc—Technique—Juvenile
  literature. | LCSH: Cartooning—Technique—Juvenile literature.
  | LCSH: Comic books, strips, etc—Juvenile literature.
Classification: LCC NC1764 .Y38 2020 | DDC j741.5/1—dc23

Library of Congress Cataloging-in-Publication Data

CIP available at the Library of Congress

LCCN: 2019057841

Crabtree Publishing Company

www.crabtreebooks.com   1-800-387-7650

Printed in the U.S.A./032020/CG20200127

**Published in Canada
Crabtree Publishing**
616 Welland Ave.
St. Catharines, Ontario
L2M 5V6

**Published in the United States
Crabtree Publishing**
PMB 59051
350 Fifth Avenue, 59th Floor
New York, New York 10118

**Published in the United Kingdom
Crabtree Publishing**
Maritime House
Basin Road North, Hove
BN41 1WR

**Published in Australia
Crabtree Publishing**
Unit 3 – 5 Currumbin Court
Capalaba
QLD 4157

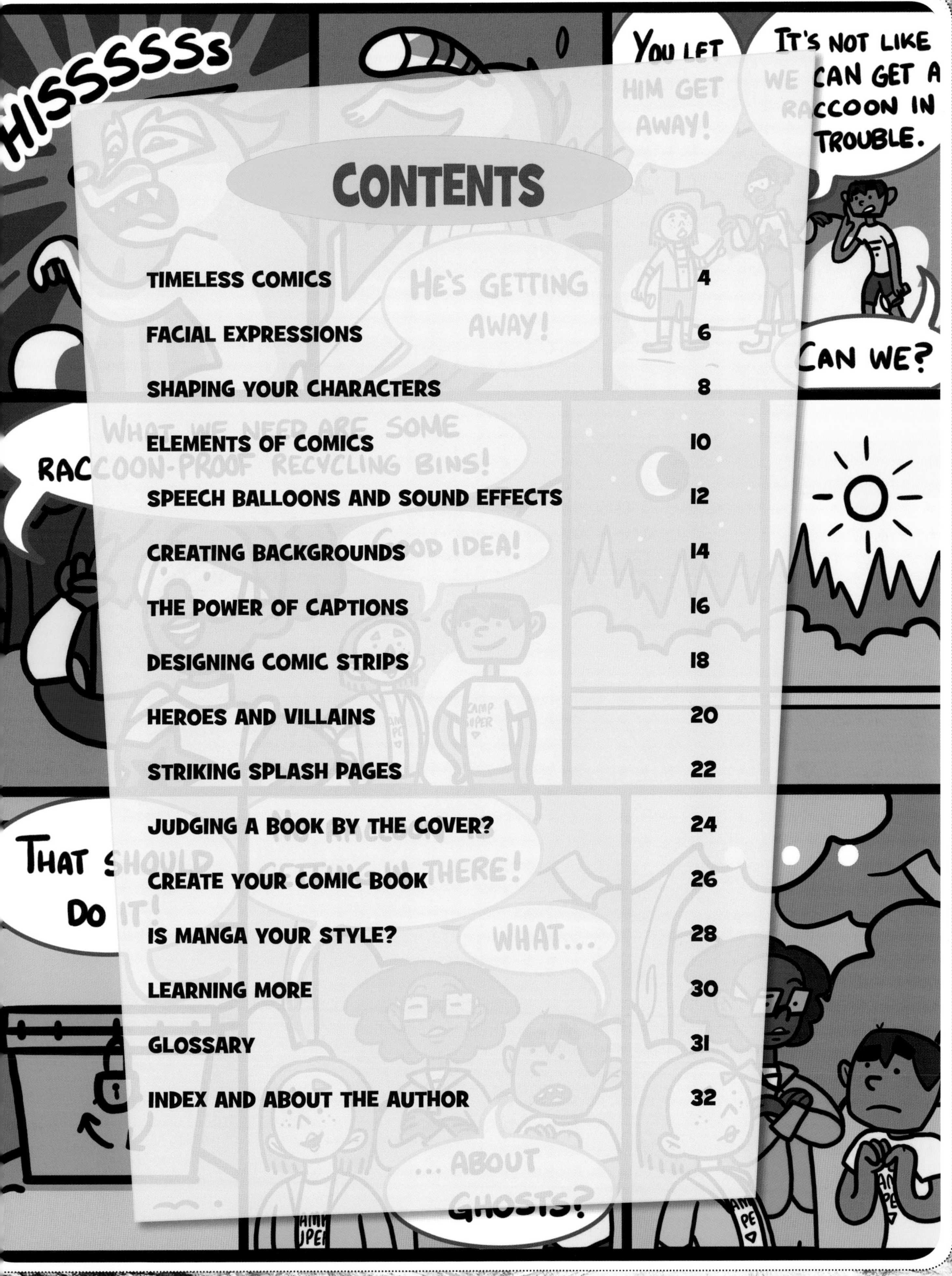
HISSSSSs
YOU LET HIM GET AWAY!
IT'S NOT LIKE WE CAN GET A RACCOON IN TROUBLE.
CAN WE?
HE'S GETTING AWAY!
WHAT WE NEED ARE SOME RACCOON-PROOF RECYCLING BINS!
GOOD IDEA!
THAT SHOULD DO IT!
WHAT...
... ABOUT GHOSTS?

CONTENTS

TIMELESS COMICS

Approach this book with a sense of adventure! It is designed to unleash the creativity within you. Do you want to create a new superhero? Would you like to draw a funny family? This book will show you all the steps in making a comic, along with examples from the **Golden Age of Comic Books**. Enjoy the process and don't worry too much about the finished product. Find your own style and run with it!

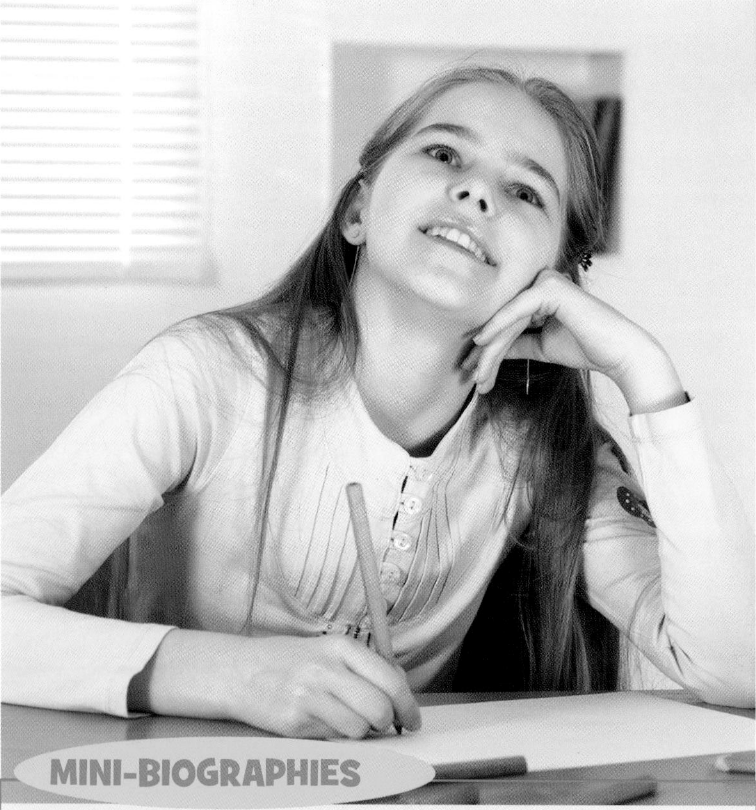

MINI-BIOGRAPHIES

Throughout the book you will find mini-biographies highlighting the work of well-known comic book artists from the Golden Age. Look at the samples of their work to get ideas for both the subjects and the **techniques** you will use for your own comics.

ORIGINS OF COMICS

People have used drawings to tell stories for thousands of years. In the 1400s, artists started using cartoon-like sketches as rough drawings for their work. By the 1700s, cartoons were being used to poke fun at people and politics. Cartoon style **exaggerates** features of people and events. The name comes from the Italian word *cartone*, which is a type of sturdy paper. American Richard Outcault was a pioneer of the modern comic strip. He first illustrated *Hogan's Alley* for a newspaper in 1895. Comic strips quickly spread worldwide in newspapers and magazines.

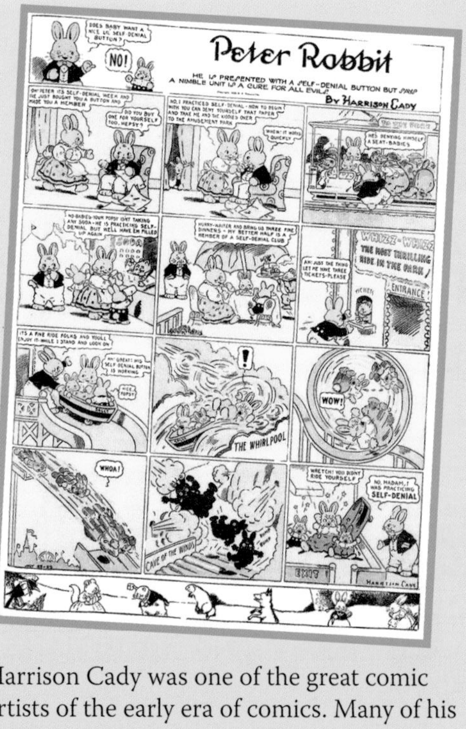
Peter Rabbit
By Harrison Cady
NO!
WOW!
THE WHIRLPOOL
WHOA!
ENTRANCE!

Harrison Cady was one of the great comic artists of the early era of comics. Many of his cartoons and comic strips featured animals. One of his best known comic strips was *Peter Rabbit*, launched in 1920. Cady wrote and drew the strip for almost 30 years.

MAIN TYPES OF COMICS

Here are some of the most popular genres, or types, of comic books today.

Superhero Comics

Superheroes fight crime in the comics with special powers that they were born with or developed.

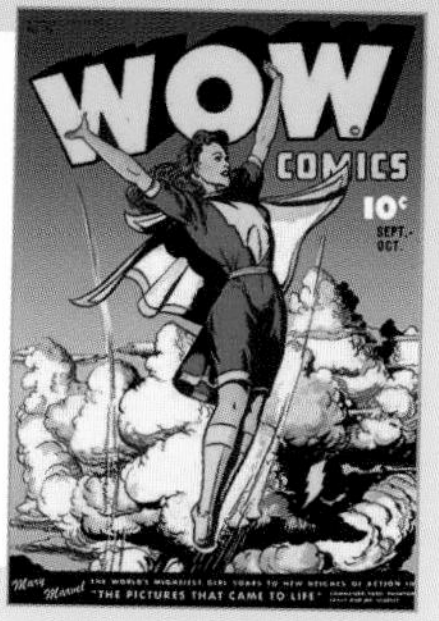
WOW
COMICS
10¢
SEPT.-OCT.

Classic Comics

When famous books like *Robin Hood* are turned into easy-to-read comic books, they are called classic comics.

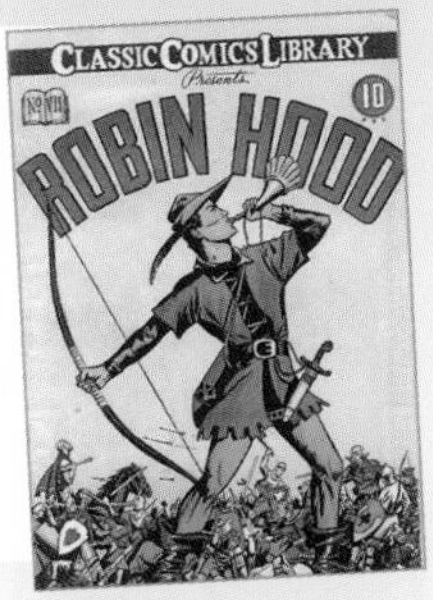
CLASSIC COMICS LIBRARY
Presents
ROBIN HOOD
10

Science Fiction Comics

Science fiction comics are usually about science in the future, space travel, and aliens. Some superhero comics are also science fiction.

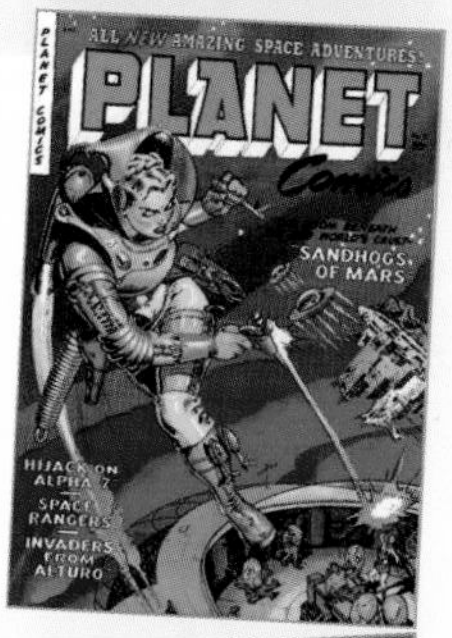
ALL NEW AMAZING SPACE ADVENTURES
PLANET
Comics
SANDHOGS OF MARS
HIJACK ON ALPHA 7
SPACE RANGERS
INVADERS FROM ALTURO

Horror Comics

When comics are designed to scare readers, they are called horror comics. Look out for zombies, vampires, and other scary creatures.

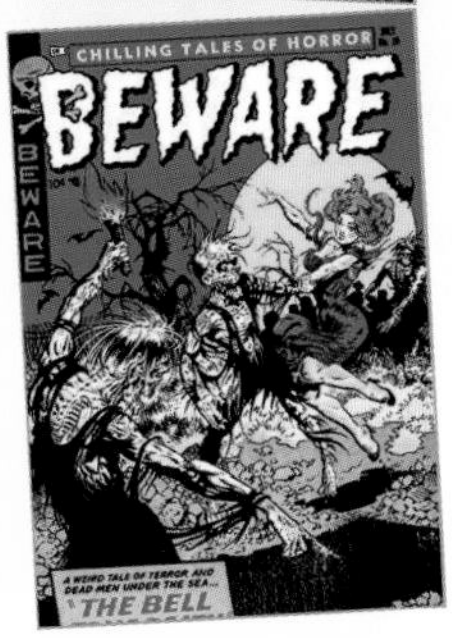
CHILLING TALES OF HORROR
BEWARE
THE BELL

Graphic Novels

The graphic novel is a recent addition to the world of comics. Graphic novels tell a longer story with grown-up **themes**. The drawings are cartoons, but they can be very elegant and detailed. Graphic novels have been popular since the 1970s.

The Golden Age of Comic Books

Comic books came along at just the right time for a troubled world. In the 1930s and 1940s, many people suffered **economic** hardships. When World War II broke out, people turned to comics to help them escape their worries. The modern comic book—and the superhero—were born, introducing characters such as Batman, Superman, Captain America, Wonder Woman, and Captain Marvel. Comics were so popular from the 1930s to the early 1950s that this period has become known as the Golden Age of Comic Books.

After the war, superheroes became less popular. Cowboys, romance, science fiction, and other **genres** became the best-selling comics. But superheroes made a big comeback in the 1960s with new heroes like Spider-Man.

While printed comics have largely been replaced in popularity today by TV, video games, and other devices, the heroes and villains from the Golden Age live on—not only in comics but in movies and TV shows, too. Keep reading to learn what it takes to become a comic artist.

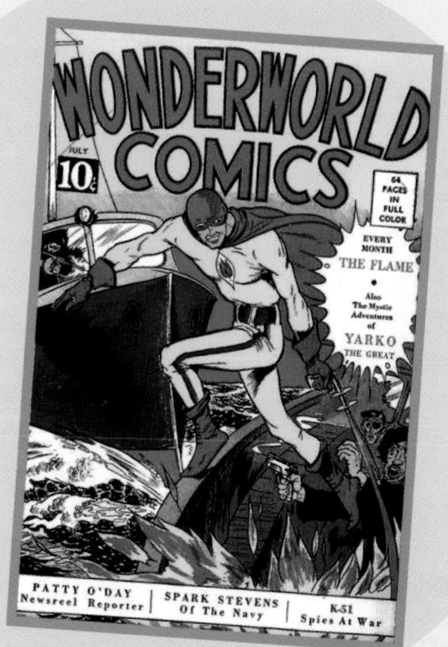
WONDERWORLD
JULY
10¢
COMICS
64 PAGES IN FULL COLOR
EVERY MONTH
THE FLAME
Also The Mystic Adventures of
YARKO THE GREAT
PATTY O'DAY Newsreel Reporter
SPARK STEVENS Of The Navy
K-51 Spies At War

The Flame was a superhero of the Golden Age, created by writer Will Eisner and artist Lou Fine in 1939.

FACIAL EXPRESSIONS

Faces tell us what comic book characters are thinking and feeling. There are even silent comics that have no words. The expressions of the characters speak for them. It's a good idea to start with faces when learning to draw comics. In this exercise, you will learn how to position and detail the parts of a face. Experiment with a lot of different looks!

For the projects in this book
You Will Need:

- Drawing paper
- Pencils
- Erasers with sharp corners
- Black ink pens and markers
- Colored pens and markers

PROJECT GUIDES

1. Make an egg shape.

2. Add a cross as shown.

3. Draw two eggs for the eyes and a smaller one for the nose.

4. Draw two small eggs for the eyeballs and a wide letter U for the mouth.

5. Erase the cross carefully. Add hair.

6. Add two small eggs for ears and dot some freckles on the face. Color your drawing.

  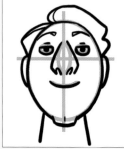  

You could draw many different faces using this technique!

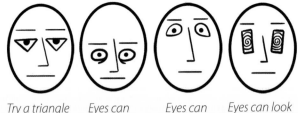

Try a triangle for eyes.

Eyes can look low.

Eyes can be high.

Eyes can look glued to the TV!

Keep mouth simple with a U.

M and O say, "Oh my!"

P is a mouth and tongue.

D and a line make a smile.

DRAWING FACE FEATURES

Now that you can make a basic face, think about the overall look of your comic characters. Do you want to keep them simple, like the egg face, or will you add a lot of details? Do you plan to color them or will they be black and white? Experiment with noses, eyes, eyebrows, hair, and ears. There are so many combinations you can use!

A triangle makes a nose.

So does a squiggle.

Some noses are small.

And some are huge!

Eyebrows show emotion.

Brows can be bold.

Arched brows show surprise.

There's no limit to brow style.

Oh dear! I'm going bald.

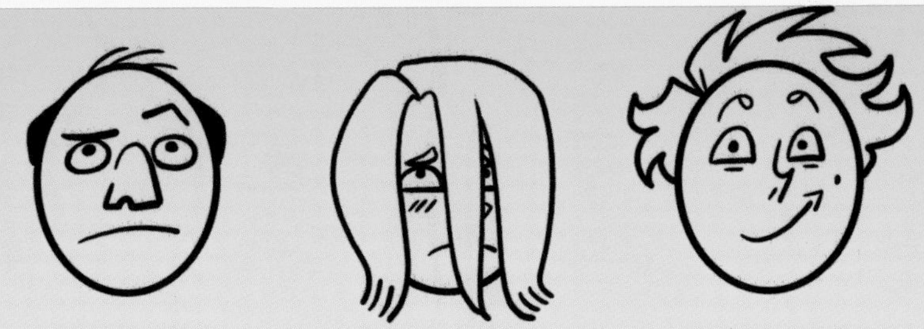

Hair, hair everywhere.

Spikes can go every which way.

Ears can be simple.

Add a Y for the inside.

Hang ears as low as you like.

DRAWING HAIR AND EARS

More details give faces more personality. Start by choosing a hairdo that tells about the character. For example, a rock star could have spikes. You can draw the outline of the hair only, or you can use a pencil to make small lines that look like hairs. Use the same technique for mustaches and beards. If the hair does not cover where the ears would be, add ears too. A basic ear is just a C shape. Use a small Y to show the inside. Then think of even more details, such as big earrings or a lot of freckles! Famous cartoonists have used everything from stick figures to highly realistic characters. It's all up to you.

DRAWING EMOTIONS

You can draw the elements of a face to show any emotion. In fact, people today use simple cartoons to show how they feel—that's what an emoji is. You could even start a face drawing from an emoji! :)

A wide U makes a happy smile.

For a sad face, flip that U upside down.

Slanted brows and a frown show anger.

Raised brows and an O mouth show surprise.

SHAPING YOUR CHARACTERS

All those faces you have been drawing are going to need bodies. In this exercise, you'll draw a body based on basic shapes. The body, like the face, should match the personality of the character. For example, an athlete should have big muscles and broad shoulders. In fact, the shoulders should be the widest part of the body. If you are drawing someone who is tubby and out of shape, the belly would be the widest part. Look through magazines and other comic books to get ideas for more body shapes.

Tip

Cartoon characters don't have to be realistic. Artists often exaggerate one or more features to make a character look extra funny or scary. Keep this in mind when designing characters!

PROJECT GUIDES

1. Make a pear shape for the **torso**. Draw a small egg shape on top for the head. Draw the eyes and eyeballs.
2. Draw the arms and legs using slightly curved lines. This looks more natural because arms and legs are not perfectly straight.
3. Add the hands, feet, and neck. Draw a mouth and nose.
4. Draw more details such as hair and clothes to bring your character to life.

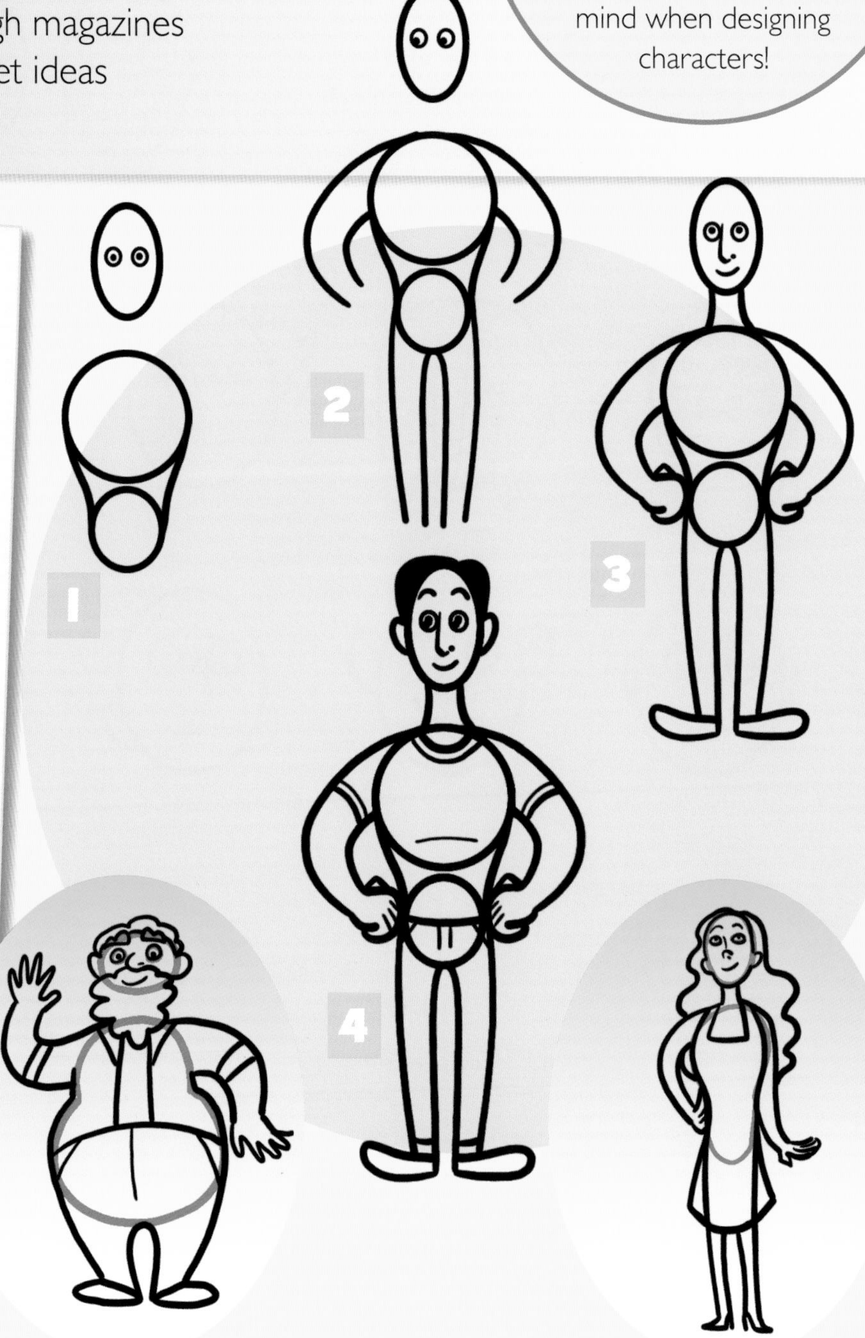

1
2
3
4

Tip

Using basic shapes will help you get started drawing characters. Ovals, circles, squares, and triangles are all useful. Look at cartoon characters and see what shapes you can find!

SKELETON TECHNIQUE

You can build on the technique of using basic shapes to create more realistic characters. The illustrations below show how to use the skeleton technique, which builds up a character's body in layers.

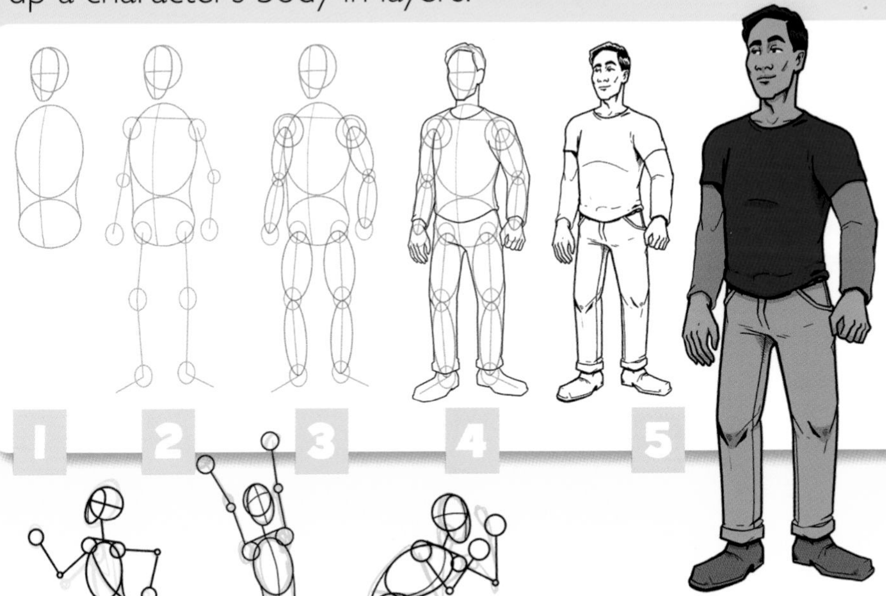
1
2
3
4
5

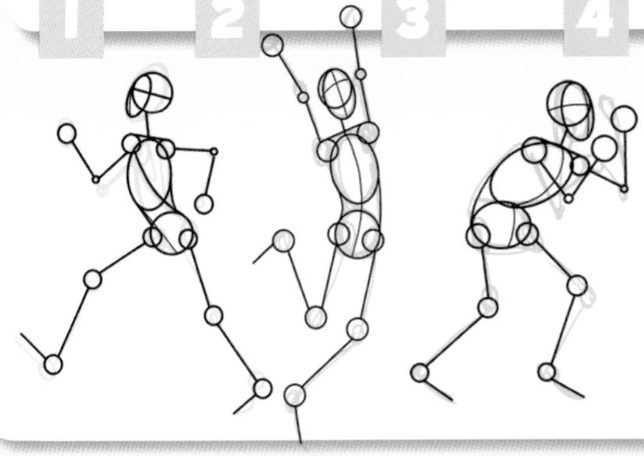

This technique is also great for drawing characters in action.

PROJECT GUIDES

1. Use a circle and a cross for the head, as you did before. Draw two ovals to outline the torso. This is just a rough sketch, so don't worry how it looks.
2. Add lines for arms and legs. Make circles to mark the shoulder, elbow, wrist, hip, knee, and ankle joints.
3. Using more ovals and lines, draw a skeleton outline of the body.
4. Outline the arms and legs with the skeleton as your guide.
5. Erase the guidelines. Add finishing touches such as hair, clothes, and color.

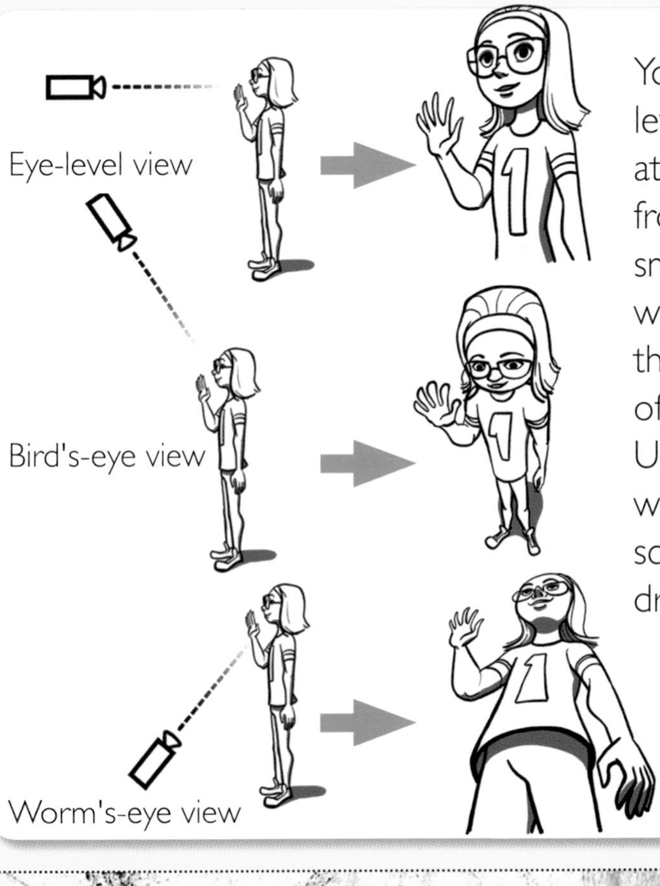
Eye-level view
Bird's-eye view
Worm's-eye view

You've been drawing characters at an eye-level view, but there are other ways to look at characters. One is the bird's-eye view from above. This makes characters seem smaller and weaker. The opposite is the worm's-eye view from below, which makes them seem larger and stronger. A third type of view is the close-up. Use the views that work best in the scene you are drawing.

Try This!

Draw a simple character at eye level. Now draw the same character from above and below. What impression does each version give?

ELEMENTS OF COMICS

The elements of a comic are the characters, background, word bubbles, and **narration**. **Layout** is the arrangement of these elements to tell the story. Layout also refers to the way the panels are arranged in relation to each other. Some comics in newspapers and magazines have just a single frame. Most comic books use six-panel pages, but will add panels when there is a lot of story to tell.

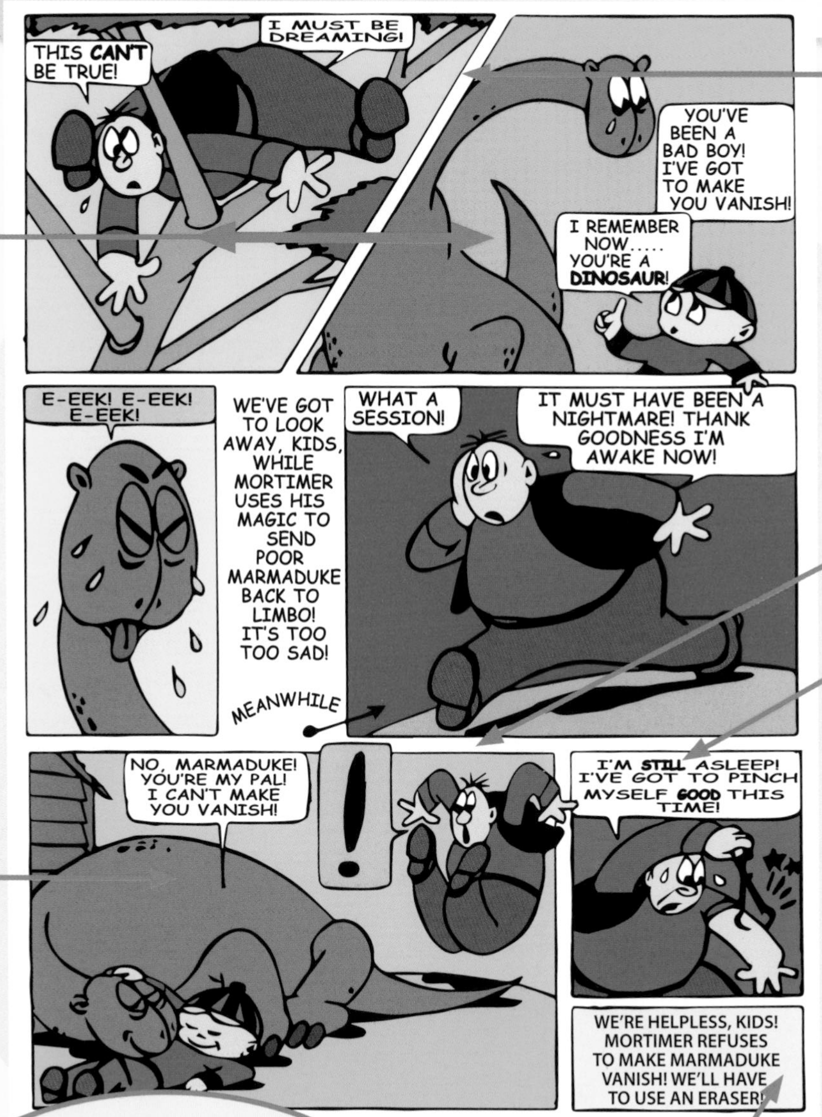

THIS CAN'T BE TRUE!
I MUST BE DREAMING!
YOU'VE BEEN A BAD BOY! I'VE GOT TO MAKE YOU VANISH!
I REMEMBER NOW..... YOU'RE A DINOSAUR!
E-EEK! E-EEK! E-EEK!
WE'VE GOT TO LOOK AWAY, KIDS, WHILE MORTIMER USES HIS MAGIC TO SEND POOR MARMADUKE BACK TO LIMBO! IT'S TOO TOO SAD!
WHAT A SESSION!
IT MUST HAVE BEEN A NIGHTMARE! THANK GOODNESS I'M AWAKE NOW!
MEANWHILE
NO, MARMADUKE! YOU'RE MY PAL! I CAN'T MAKE YOU VANISH!
!
I'M STILL ASLEEP! I'VE GOT TO PINCH MYSELF GOOD THIS TIME!
WE'RE HELPLESS, KIDS! MORTIMER REFUSES TO MAKE MARMADUKE VANISH! WE'LL HAVE TO USE AN ERASER!

Tier

A row across of panels is called a tier. This sample comic page has two-panel tiers.

Panel

The squares or rectangles on each page are called panels. A panel contains just one scene of the story. A panel may also be called a frame.

Gutter

The gutter is the white space between panels. Gutters give readers the sense that time has passed from one scene to the next, even if it is only a few seconds. They help the eye move from scene to scene.

Speech Balloons

Speech balloons, also called word balloons, show what the characters are saying and thinking. Each bubble has a tail that points to the speaker. If the outline is rippled like a cloud, the bubble is showing thoughts rather than spoken words.

Caption

Comics may need a narrator to explain things and move the story along. The narration appears in a box called a caption. Captions usually are colored to set them apart from the panel.

Tip

Keep a balance between words and action in your layout. You don't want to bog the action down with word bubbles! If a character has a lot to say, you may need more than one panel for it. If a lot of characters need to speak, consider combining two or more panels into one larger space or do a splash page (see page 22).

I KNOW IT WAS YOU WHO INVENTED THE WHEEL. FRED JUST SAYS HE HAS SOME REALLY GOOD IDEAS FOR WHAT TO DO WITH IT.

SO, WHAT DOES THE NEWSPAPER SAY?
THE PAP
DON'T TELL ME ABOUT EVERYTHING, JUST THE FUN STUFF ... WELL?
YOU REALLY THINK A DOG CAN READ?

One or More Panels?

Some cartoons, especially in magazines, are a single panel, like the cartoon at left. Single-panel comics usually have a caption below and no **dialogue**, or a line or two of short dialogue. Newspaper comics usually have three or four panels with more room for talking.

GET GOING, TIM!!
I JUST CAN'T RUN OUT ON YOU, TERROR!
HELP!
I HATE TO SEE RATS RUNNING AROUND LOOSE IN THE JUNGLE!
YOU HELPED PILOT THE PLANE, DIDN'T YOU?
OOOFF!
WE SURE STIRRED THINGS UP THAT TIME, TERROR!
NOW LET'S STIR OURSELVES UP... AND GET A MOVE ON!
A STARTLING DISCOVERY...
GREAT SCOTT, TIM! LOOK AT THAT!!
THEY LOOK LIKE ATOMIC BOMBS!!
I'M SURE THEY ARE, TIM! BUT -- I'M NOT SURE I KNOW JUST WHAT THE PURPOSE OF THAT PLATFORM IS!
PERHAPS I CAN ENLIGHTEN YOU, TERROR! BUT--I MUST ASK YOU TO KEEP YOUR HANDS RAISED WHILE WE TALK!
PERMIT ME TO INTRODUCE MY-SELF! MY NAME IS JOHN REECE. AND I DEAL IN PRODUCTS OF DESTRUCTION! TO THE HIGHEST BIDDER -- I OFFER THE WORLD ON AN ATOMIC PLATTER!!

Panel Sizes

Comics may have typical sizes, but there are no limits. A more important panel can be larger than a less important one. One of the panels can be divided as in the example at left. The panels can be designed to match the flow of the story.

Try This!

Think of a joke that you like to tell. If you were making a comic based on that joke, would it be a single panel? Would you need three or more panels to tell the joke? Draw a simple cartoon based on the joke.

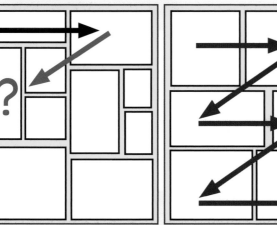

?
Wrong grid

Right grid

Panel Grids

Comic book artists mostly use the six- or nine-panel format because they do not want to overwhelm readers. A comic should be easy to follow from left to right, then down the page. If there are too many small panels, it will be unclear which way the eye should go.

MEDDLE WITH ME, HUH-- AIEEEEE!
SORRY TO DISAPPOINT YOU, HEEL!
NOW FOR A FRESH DIET OF KNUCKLES!
IT'S PYROMAN! MOW HIM DOWN!
BOOM
NOTHING LIKE EXERCISE TO KEEP HEALTHY!
LEMME OUTA HERE! DAT FELLA'S NOT HUMAN--!
WAM
WELL, WELL! SHORTY FIELDS! YOU'RE GOING FAST. BOY! WHO DRILLED YOU?
DAWSON, EH? HE'S AN OUT OF TOWN RACKETEER! A NASTY LAD, THEY TELL ME!
SHORTY'S DONE FOR-- HE SAID IT WAS THE DAWSON GANG!
GEE--IT IS PYROMAN! WOW!
WE'VE GOT TO PUT A STOP TO THIS GANG WARFARE!
SEE--I TOLD YA I SAW HIM!

POOR MARMADUKE WANTED SOME MILK!
MY EYES SEE THINGS, BUT MY BRAINS DON'T BELIEVE 'EM!
IF HE'S SOLID I CAN HIT HIM!
SOCK
STOP TEASING MARMADUKE, POP!
OH! OH! POP IS SO MAD HE'LL RAISE THE ROOF!
FAREWELL! IT'S THE END OF THE WORLD!

Panel Shapes

Panels don't have to be squares or rectangles. Irregular panels alert readers that something important is happening. Another variation is to put a circular drawing inside a square panel, or you can draw the panel as a circle, star, or free-form shape.

SPEECH BALLOONS AND SOUND EFFECTS

How do you make sounds in a silent medium? Artists have faced this challenge for centuries. Paintings in the Middle Ages and Renaissance used ribbons with words in them. True word balloons became widespread in comics after Rudolph Dirks began using them in *The Katzenjammer Kids*. You can use the size and shape of letters and the outline of the balloon to show emotions or sounds. For example, small letters are a whisper, and big, bold letters are a roar! Look at some comics to get ideas for word balloons.

LISTEN TO ME, I AM SPEAKING HERE!
LET'S DO IT TOGETHER.

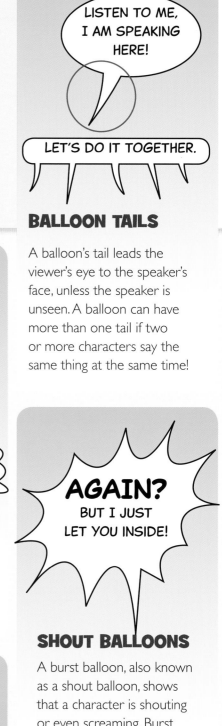

BALLOON TAILS

A balloon's tail leads the viewer's eye to the speaker's face, unless the speaker is unseen. A balloon can have more than one tail if two or more characters say the same thing at the same time!

WAIT FOR ME!
I NEED TO CATCH MY BREATH.
FINE, I'LL WAIT ...
I'M COMING!
... BUT DON'T TAKE TOO LONG!

JOINING BALLOONS WITH CONNECTORS

A double balloon with a connecting bridge has two meanings. In the first example, one character is talking, but saying two different things. The second example shows two speakers having a conversation.

THOUGHT BALLOONS

Thought balloons look like a cloud and have bubbles for a tail. They should point to the character's head where all that thinking is going on.

I THINK WE SHOULD JOIN IN AND HELP WITH THE CLEANUP ...

AGAIN?
BUT I JUST LET YOU INSIDE!

SHOUT BALLOONS

A burst balloon, also known as a shout balloon, shows that a character is shouting or even screaming. Burst balloons have jagged edges and bold lines. Important words may be enlarged, darkened, or underlined.

ROUGH BALLOONS

Rough-looking edges and letters are often used when a monster is speaking.

I AM THE CAVE MONSTER AND ONE DAY I WILL GET YOU!

CREATING SOUND EFFECTS WITH WORDS

Loud noises won't stay inside a balloon! They are drawn with big, bright letters and a lot of special effects. Experiment with creating your own sound effects based on the examples below. There are no strict rules to follow, use your imagination and have fun with it!

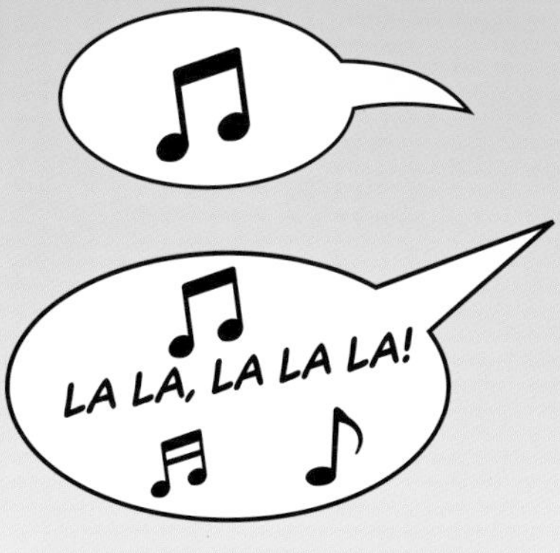
LA LA, LA LA!

MUSIC AND SINGING

A musical note indicates whistling or music playing that has no words. For singing, words are put in slanted letters, called ***italics***, along with musical notes.

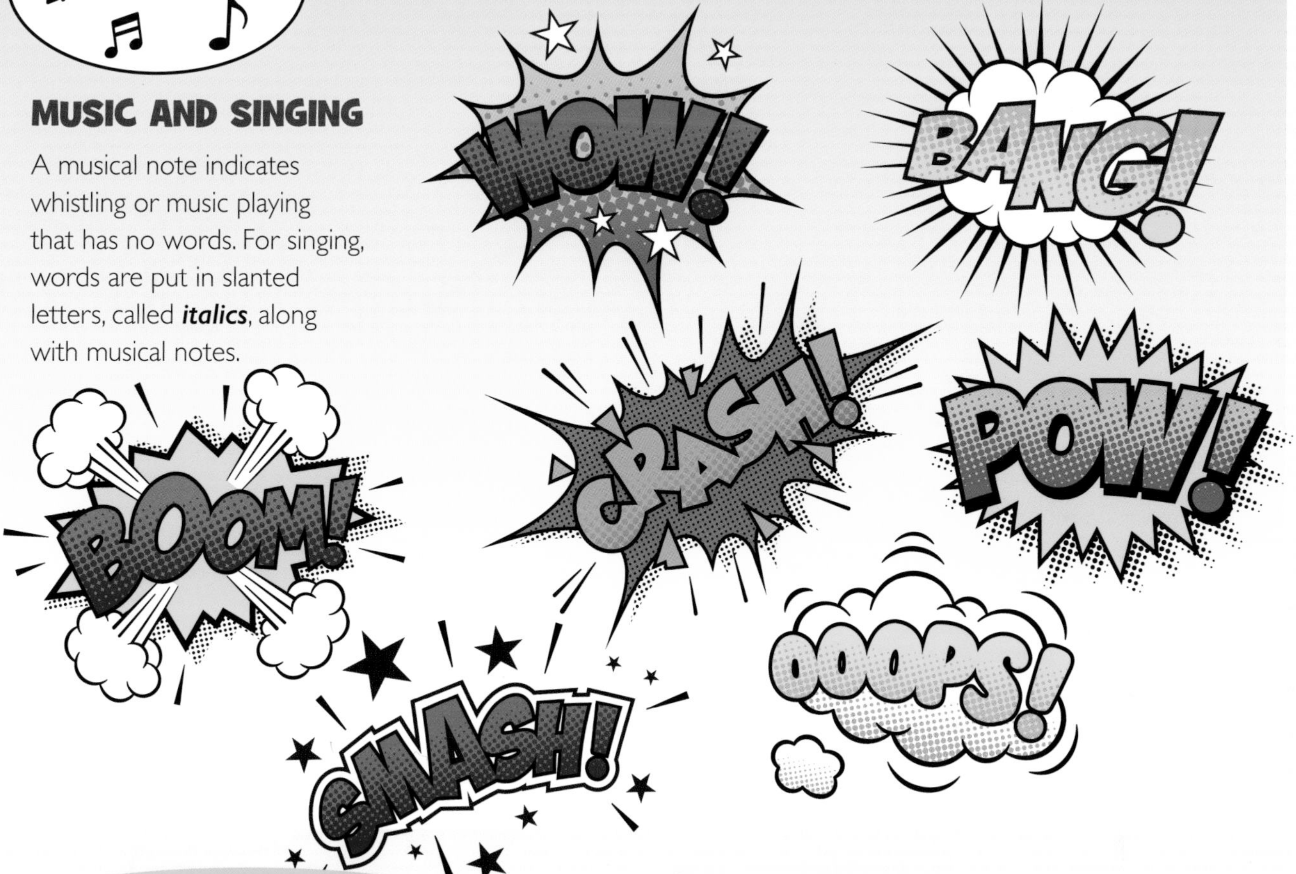
WOW!
BANG!
CRASH!
POW!
BOOM!
OOOPS!
SMASH!

RUDOLPH DIRKS

(1877 – 1968) United States

The Katzenjammer Kids was one of the first comic strips. It was also one of the first to use word balloons and a series of panels to tell a story. In 1897, cartoonist Rudolph Dirks created the characters Hans and Fritz, two boys who love to pull pranks. Their adventures have been featured in newspapers ever since! At 113 years, that's a record run for a comic strip. Several artists have drawn the strip over all those years, but Dirks is considered a pioneer whose work helped to pave the way for the Golden Age.

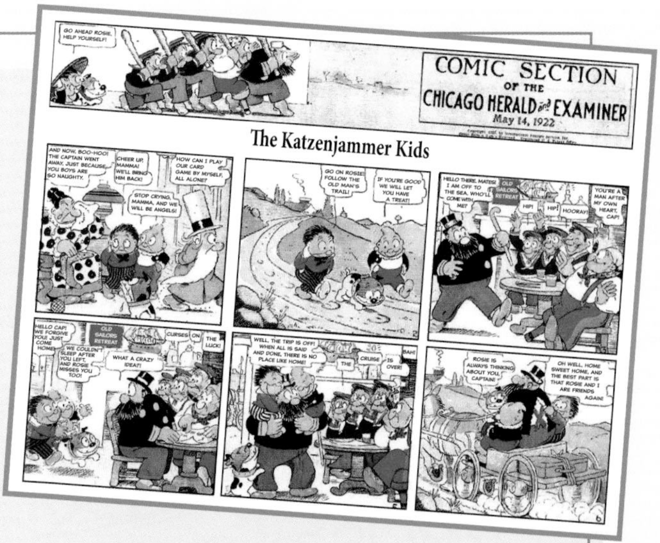
GO AHEAD ROSIE, HELP YOURSELF!
COMIC SECTION OF THE CHICAGO HERALD and EXAMINER
May 14, 1922
The Katzenjammer Kids
AND NOW, BOO-HOO! THE CAPTAIN WENT AWAY, JUST BECAUSE YOU BOYS ARE SO NAUGHTY.
CHEER UP, MAMMA! WE'LL BRING HIM BACK!
HOW CAN I PLAY OUR CARD GAME BY MYSELF, ALL ALONE?
STOP CRYING, MAMMA, AND WE WILL BE ANGELS!
GO ON ROSIE! FOLLOW THE OLD MAN'S TRAIL!
IF YOU'RE GOOD WE WILL LET YOU HAVE A TREAT!
HELLO THERE, MATES! I AM OFF TO THE SEA. WHO'LL COME WITH ME?
OLD SAILORS RETREAT
HIP!
HIP!
HOORAY!
YOU'RE A MAN AFTER MY OWN HEART, CAP!
HELLO CAP! WE FORGIVE YOU! JUST COME HOME!
OLD SAILORS RETREAT
WE COULDN'T SLEEP AFTER YOU LEFT, AND ROSIE MISSES YOU TOO!
WHAT A CRAZY IDEA?!
CURSES
ON
THE LUCK!
WELL, THE TRIP IS OFF! WHEN ALL IS SAID AND DONE, THERE IS NO PLACE LIKE HOME!
THE
CRUISE
IS OVER!
BAH!
ROSIE IS ALWAYS THINKING ABOUT YOU, CAPTAIN!
OH WELL, HOME SWEET HOME, AND THE BEST PART IS THAT ROSIE AND I ARE FRIENDS AGAIN!

This *Katzenjammer Kids* comic strip was drawn in 1922.

CREATING BACKGROUNDS

Every action happens against a background, such as in a kid's room or on an alien planet. Some comics create backgrounds with just a few lines and shapes. Others have more detail, but there is no need to go overboard. You don't need to draw every tree to show a forest. Build up your background skills with these two exercises.

1

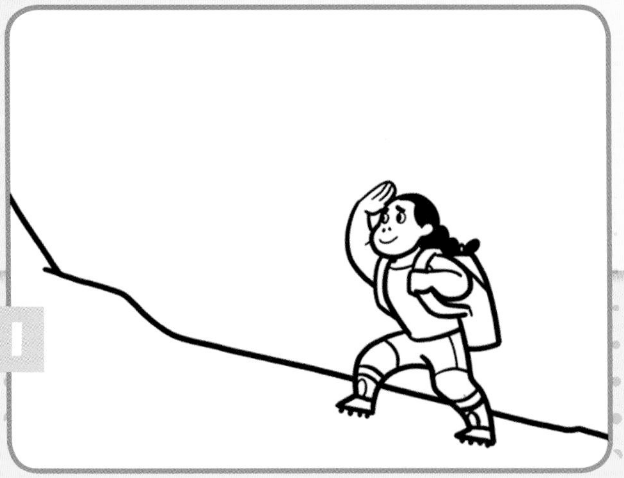

2

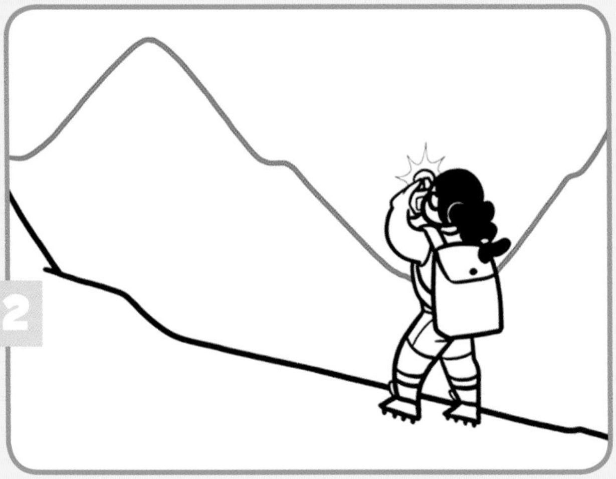

3

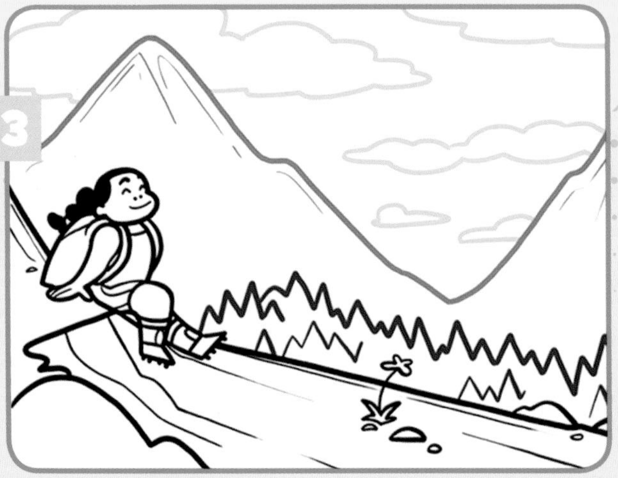

PROJECT GUIDES

1. Imagine a hiker walking uphill. Use a thick line to show how the ground goes up.
2. Draw a mountain peak and a valley in the background.
3. Add clouds, rocks, flowers, and bushes.

Tip

Use just enough detail to give the feel of a background. It's hard to follow a cluttered panel, like the one below.

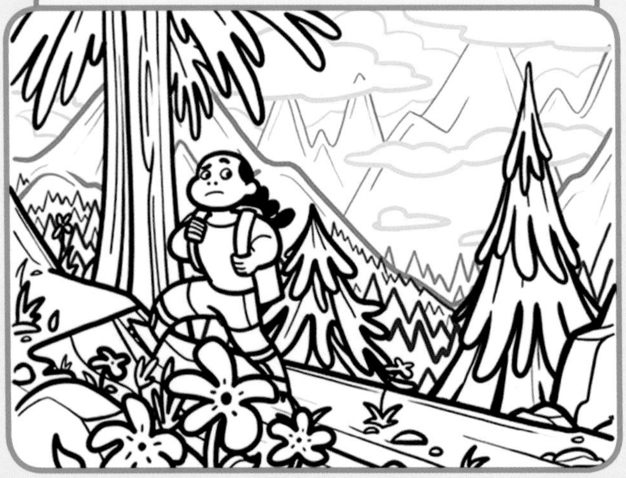

KEEP IT IN PERSPECTIVE

Perspective is a way of drawing a **two-dimensional** scene so that it seems to have depth, as well as height and width. With perspective, you can create a 3-D look on a flat piece of paper. To do this, you need to make a vanishing point. This is the farthest point away that things can be seen. Everything in a drawing with perspective falls along a line coming out of the vanishing point. Things at the front of the line appear larger than those at the back. Try drawing a scene with different vanishing points. How does your drawing change?

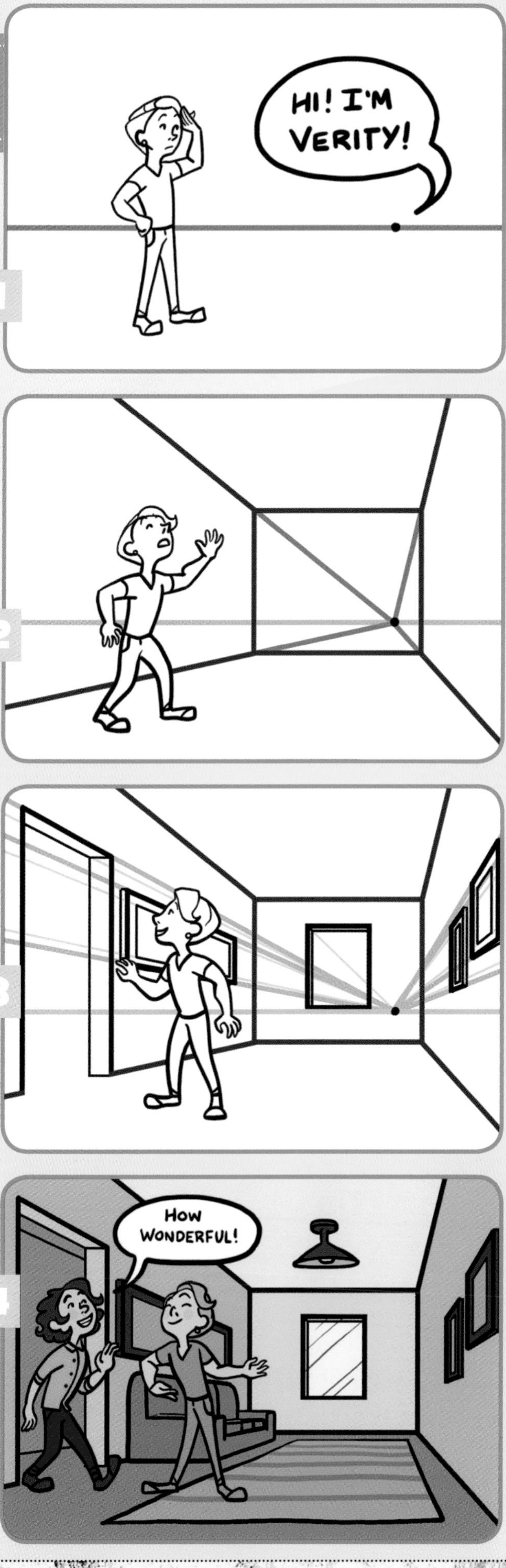
HI! I'M VERITY!
HOW WONDERFUL!

PROJECT GUIDES

1. Draw a line across a cartoon panel. This is called the **horizon line**. Make a dot to mark your vanishing point. For this exercise, we'll call it Verity the Vanishing Point.
2. Draw four lines from Verity to the edges of the page making triangles, as shown. Make Verity the point of each triangle.
3. Use the triangles as guides to draw the walls, floor, windows, and door. Then you can erase Verity and the triangle lines that are not in your drawing.
4. Add furniture and characters. Color your panel.

THE POWER OF CAPTIONS

Captions are words that appear in a box at the top or bottom of a comic panel. A character may do the talking in a caption, but a narrator or author also could be speaking. Artists will often put the narrator's words in a box with a different color background to identify it as the narrator's voice. (See an example on page 10.) The comics on this page show how captions determine the meaning for a comic. Just by changing the caption, you can completely change what's going on in the cartoon from the character's **motivation,** to the point of the joke.

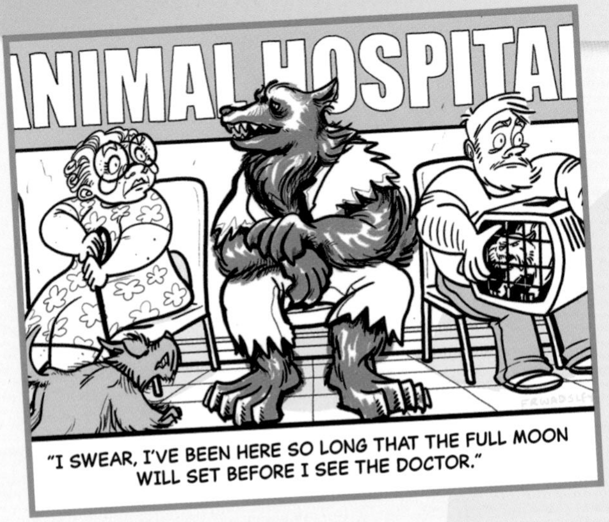
ANIMAL HOSPITAL
"I SWEAR, I'VE BEEN HERE SO LONG THAT THE FULL MOON WILL SET BEFORE I SEE THE DOCTOR."

A caption should be clear in both the meaning and the type of lettering used.

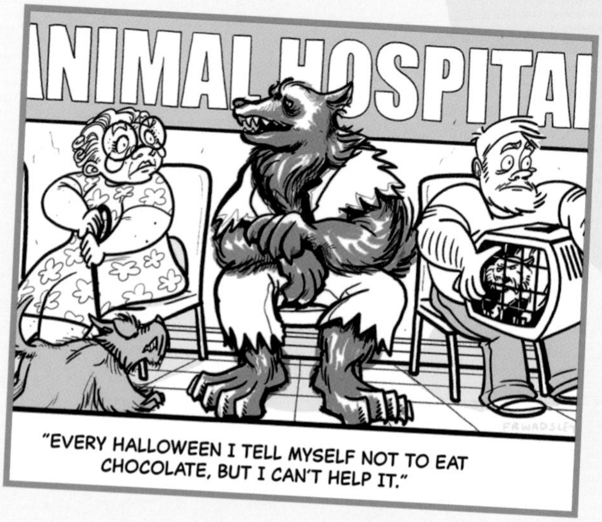
ANIMAL HOSPITAL
"EVERY HALLOWEEN I TELL MYSELF NOT TO EAT CHOCOLATE, BUT I CAN'T HELP IT."

In each pair of captions on this page, the bottom one has a whole new meaning.

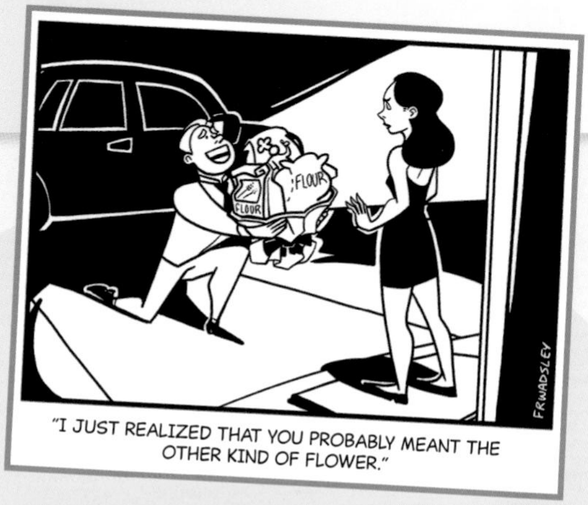
FLOUR
FRWADSLEY
"I JUST REALIZED THAT YOU PROBABLY MEANT THE OTHER KIND OF FLOWER."

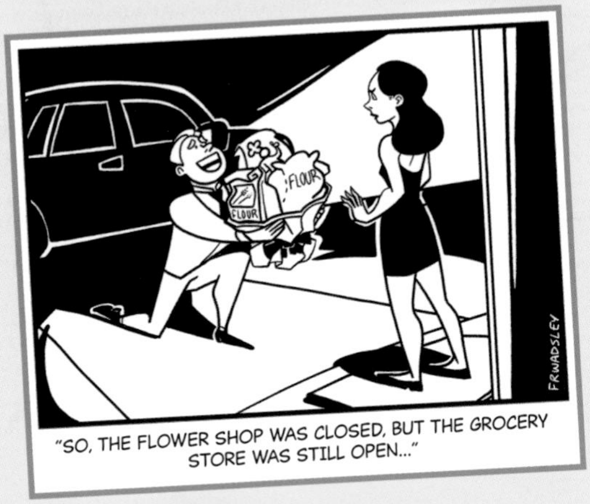
FLOUR
FRWADSLEY
"SO, THE FLOWER SHOP WAS CLOSED, BUT THE GROCERY STORE WAS STILL OPEN..."

Tip

Ideas for cartoons are everywhere! It could be your pet, your sports team, your hobby, or your family. If you have a great idea, write it down in a notepad or journal. You may end up with a whole list of funny ideas to choose from!

FUNNY BUSINESS

Many cartoons are designed to be humorous, but humor can be tricky. Not everyone laughs at the same things! One form of humor that cartoonists often use is slapstick. Slapstick is silly and physical, like the clown throwing a pie in the comic strip below. It is one of the oldest and most reliable ways to make people laugh. The name comes from an actual stick that comic actors would use to slap each other in Italy in the 1500s!

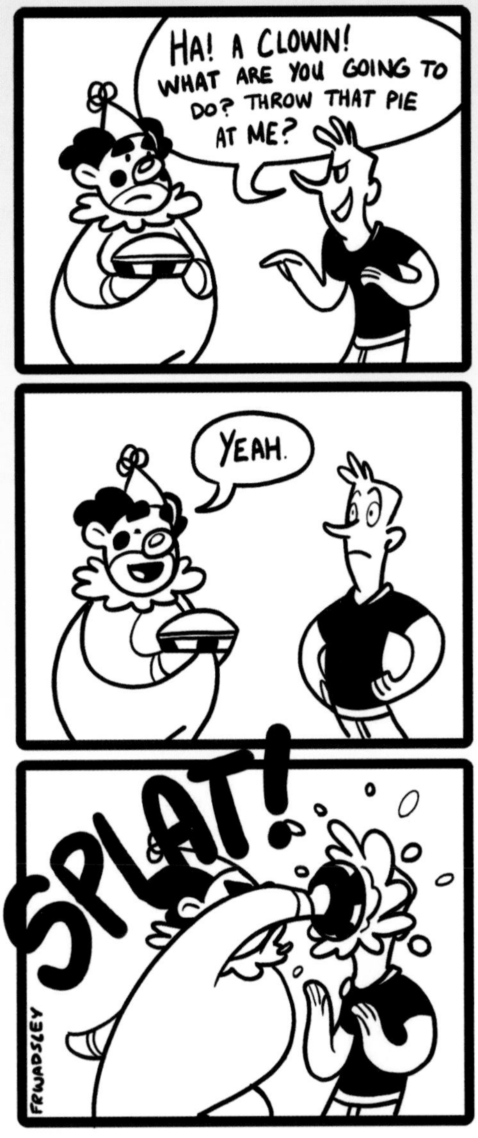
HA! A CLOWN! WHAT ARE YOU GOING TO DO? THROW THAT PIE AT ME?
YEAH.
SPLAT!
FRWADSLEY

Try This!

When comics tell a joke, the last line is a funny twist called the punch line. You can do the same thing with a multi-panel cartoon. Think of a funny punch line and create a comic for it!

JIMMY FRISE

(1891 – 1948) Canada

Some humor is sharp, and some is sweet. Canadian cartoonist Jimmy Frise took a sweet look at the humor in country life. His most famous comic, *Birdseye Center,* was set in a small town like the one where he grew up. He said it was based on life in "any Canadian village." The lovable villagers had funny **quirks** that endeared them to millions of readers. Frise started drawing the strip in the 1920s and it was extremely successful. He was honored by the Province of Ontario for helping to preserve and celebrate its heritage.

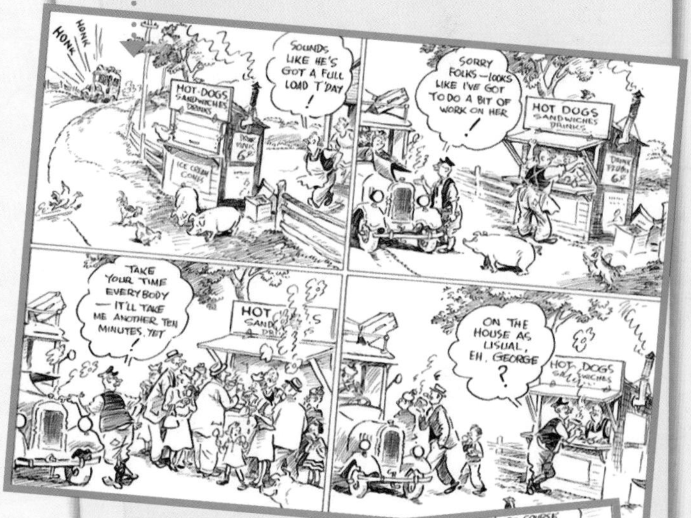
HONK HONK
HOT-DOGS SANDWICHES DRINKS
ICE CREAM CONES
SOUNDS LIKE HE'S GOT A FULL LOAD T'DAY !
SORRY FOLKS—LOOKS LIKE I'VE GOT TO DO A BIT OF WORK ON HER !
HOT DOGS SANDWICHES DRINKS
TAKE YOUR TIME EVERYBODY —IT'LL TAKE ME ANOTHER TEN MINUTES, YET !
ON THE HOUSE AS USUAL, EH, GEORGE ?
HOT DOGS

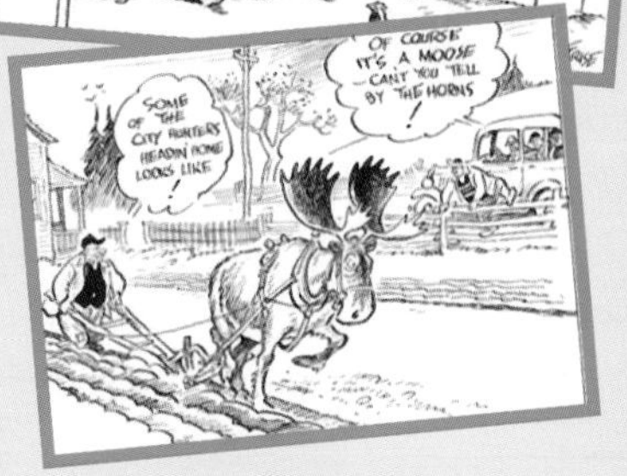
SOME OF THE CITY HUNTERS HEADIN' HOME LOOKS LIKE !
OF COURSE IT'S A MOOSE —CAN'T YOU TELL BY THE HORNS !

Among the funny characters in *Birdseye Center* was Foghorn, a pet moose.

DESIGNING COMIC STRIPS

Unlike single panels, which show only one moment, a comic strip is a line of panels that show a story unfolding. Comic strips can go across a page or up and down. Many strips have four panels, but the number can vary. In the early-to-mid 1900s, every newspaper had multiple pages of black and white comics on weekdays and color comics on Sundays. Another name for these pages was the funny papers, or funnies. In this exercise, you will create a funny comic strip with four panels.

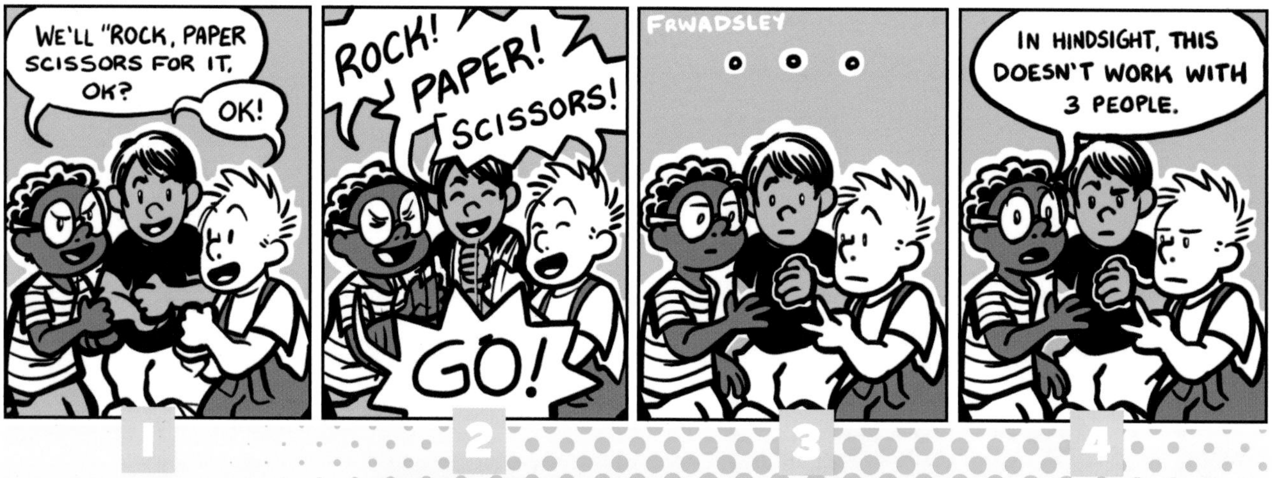
WE'LL "ROCK, PAPER SCISSORS FOR IT, OK?
OK!
1
ROCK!
PAPER!
SCISSORS!
GO!
2
FRWADSLEY
3
IN HINDSIGHT, THIS DOESN'T WORK WITH 3 PEOPLE.
4

PROJECT GUIDES

1 Introduce the characters.

2 Continue the action.

3 Create a twist to surprise readers.

4 And finish it off with a funny ending!

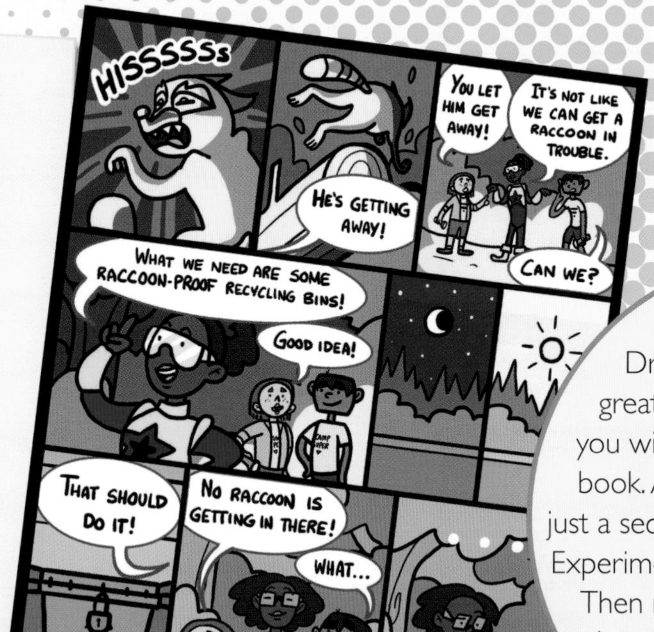
HISSSSSs
HE'S GETTING AWAY!
YOU LET HIM GET AWAY!
IT'S NOT LIKE WE CAN GET A RACCOON IN TROUBLE.
CAN WE?
WHAT WE NEED ARE SOME RACCOON-PROOF RECYCLING BINS!
GOOD IDEA!
THAT SHOULD DO IT!
NO RACCOON IS GETTING IN THERE!
WHAT...
... ABOUT GHOSTS?

Tip

Drawing a comic strip is a great way to practice the skills you will need for your own comic book. A comic book page is really just a sequence of several comic strips. Experiment with ideas and characters. Then make sure your final panels have **clean lines**, and the word balloons are clear and easy to read.

ANIMAL FUNNIES

Artists often have a preference for the kind of characters they tell their stories through. Some use only human characters, some use human and animal characters together, and some tell the story from the point of view of animals. Experiment with drawing each kind to find out which approach works best for you.

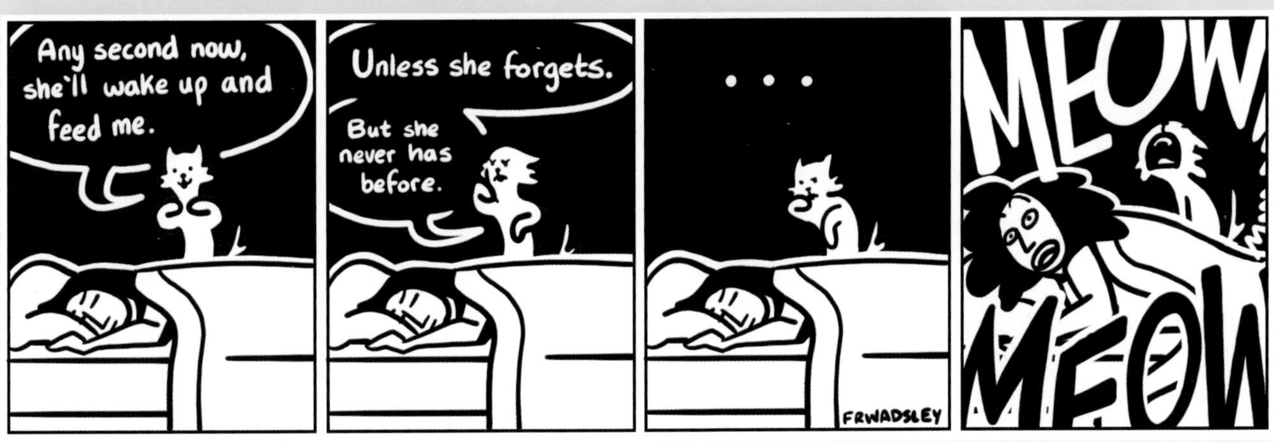
Any second now, she'll wake up and feed me.
Unless she forgets.
But she never has before.
• • •
MEOW
MEOW
FRWADSLEY

In comic strips, some funny animals act and think just like people. Others are more like pets in real life. Sometimes the human-like animals have pets of their own!

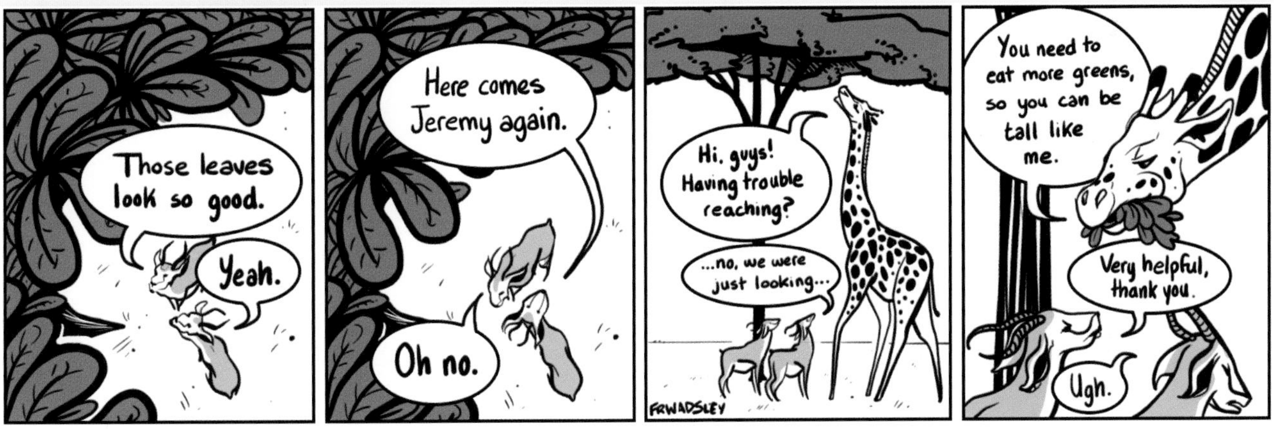
Those leaves look so good.
Yeah.
Here comes Jeremy again.
Oh no.
Hi, guys! Having trouble reaching?
...no, we were just looking...
FRWADSLEY
You need to eat more greens, so you can be tall like me.
Very helpful, thank you.
Ugh.

People love funny animals—think of cat videos—and funny stories. Put the two together and you have a funny animal comic strip. This genre has been popular since at least 1892. Characters such as Snoopy and Mickey Mouse have become all-time favorites worldwide. Comic strip animals are often used to poke fun at people and teach a lesson. The use of animals in this way is called an **allegory.**

Try This!

Try to create a series of funny pictures that explains how animals actually see the events that happen around them. Try drawing both types of animal comic strips. Make one a story about animals doing funny things. Make the other an allegory that is funny, but also teaches a lesson about becoming a better person.

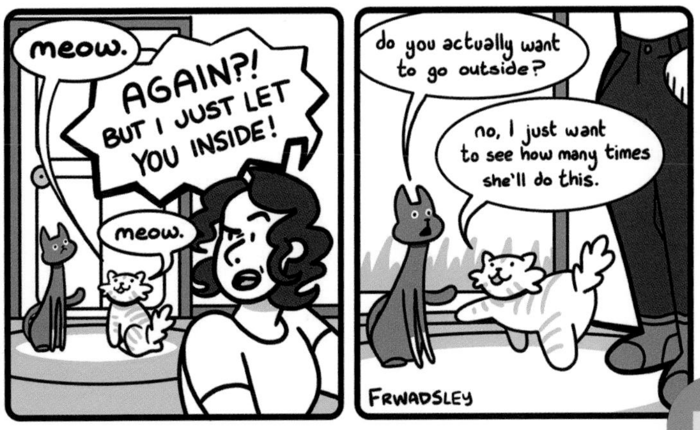
meow.
AGAIN?! BUT I JUST LET YOU INSIDE!
meow.
do you actually want to go outside?
no, I just want to see how many times she'll do this.
FRWADSLEY

HEROES AND VILLAINS

Comics are full of superheroes because people like to see good triumph over evil. Tales of great heroes have been popular since ancient times. Some ancient heroes, such as Hercules, even ended up getting their own TV shows and movies in modern times. Of course, all those heroes need super villains to challenge them. Super villains are smart and tricky. They think they are the real star of the story, and they want all the attention. Try drawing your own superhero and super villain.

Did you know?

Batman has been trying to stop the Joker since 1940! Both were created during the Golden Age of Comics, and they have stayed golden, with new movies and TV shows about them coming out all the time.

2

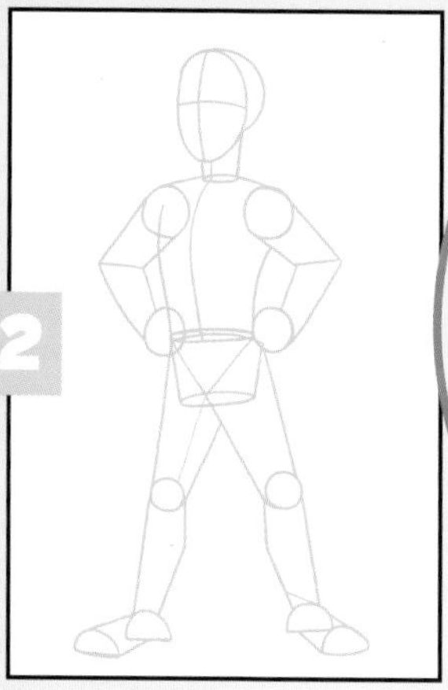

3

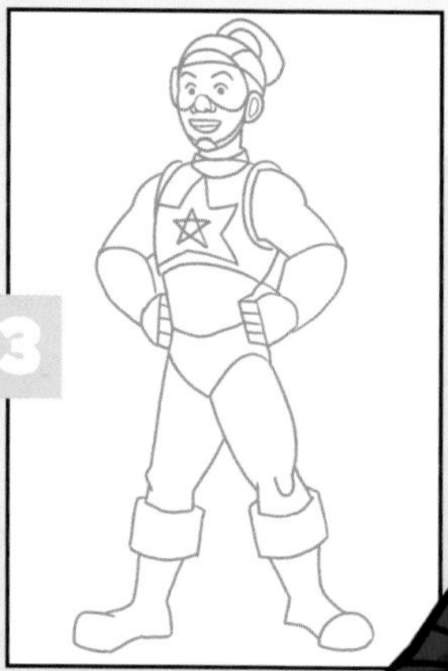

4

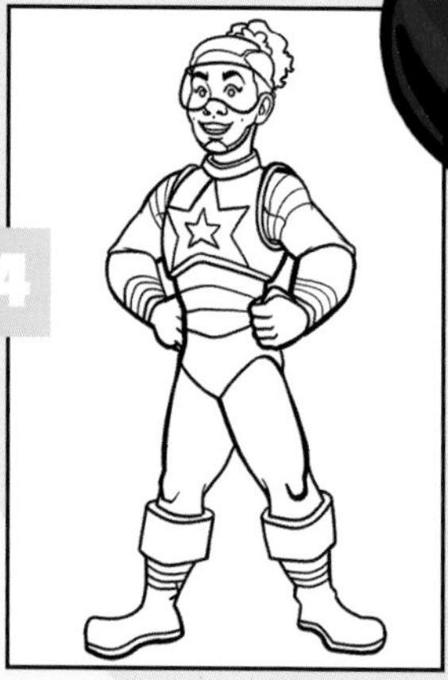

5

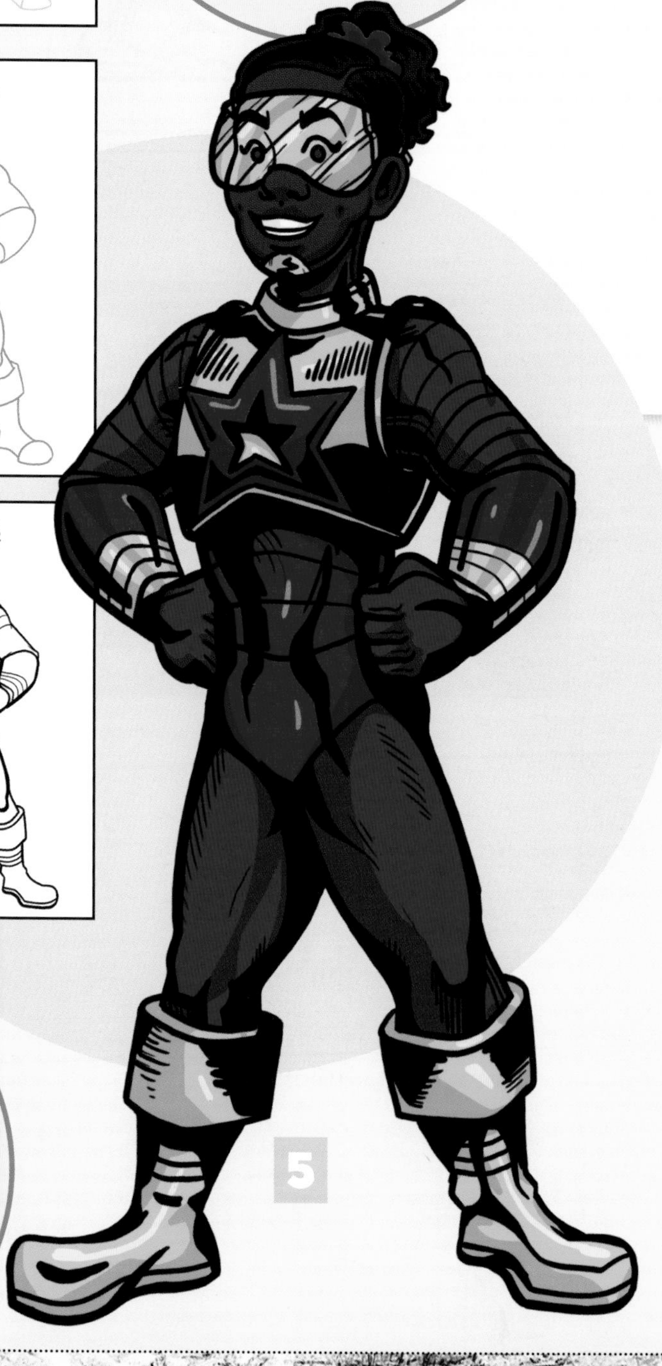

PROJECT GUIDES

1. Come up with a superhero and a villain. Decide what they will look like and give them catchy names.
2. Use the stick figure and skeleton techniques on pages 8-9 to draw your superhero.
3. Add details such as a costume and hairdo.
4. Check your drawing carefully. It's fine to make changes. When you are happy with it, go over it with clean lines. Erase the guidelines.
5. Add color to your superhero.
6. Repeat the steps for your villain.

Try this!

Create an animal superhero, too. It could be a caped cat or a dog from outer space! Your super-pet can be a hero on its own or a sidekick for one of your superheroes.

TURNING TO THE DARK SIDE

At the start of the Golden Age, comic book heroes fought gangsters, bank robbers, and other everyday criminals. No one is sure who created the first super villain. By 1940, though, comic book artists were turning to super villains to make their stories more thrilling. People may like to see good triumph, but they also like a good scare along the way! Some super villains have superpowers. Others are evil geniuses. Either way, characters like the Joker and Lex Luthor have become just as popular with readers as Batman and Superman.

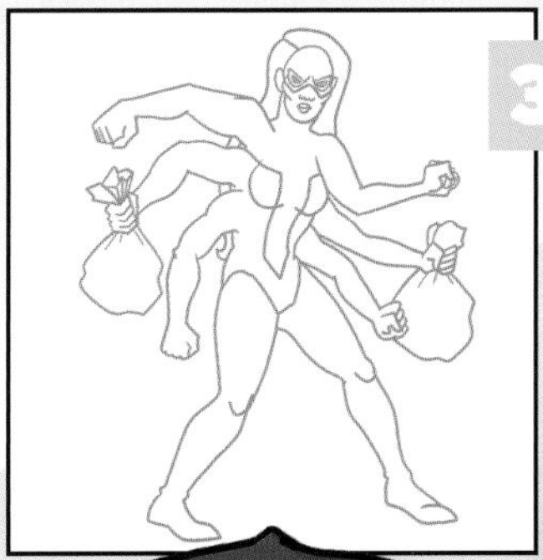

3

4

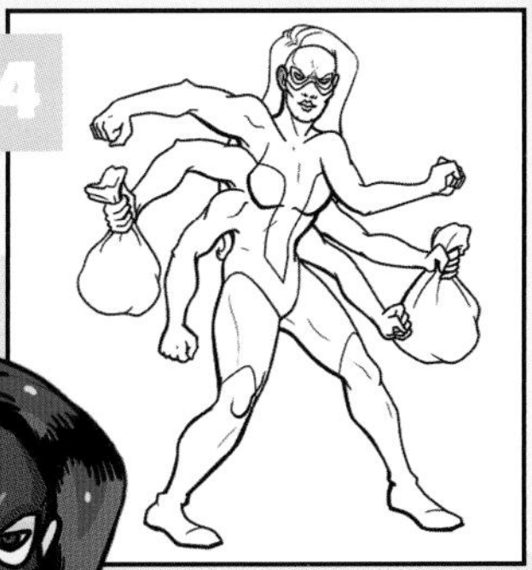

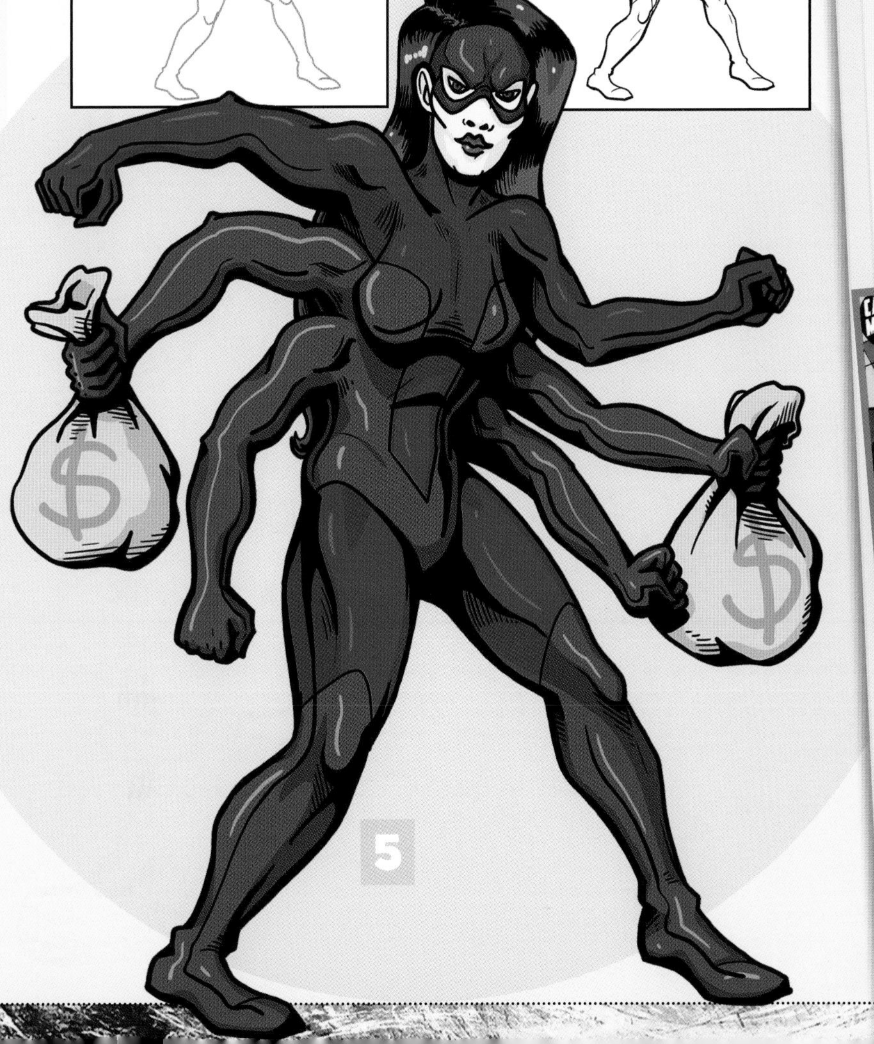

5

C. C. BECK

(1910 – 1989) United States

If you want to see clean lines in a comic book, look at the work of Golden Age artist C.C. (Charles Clarence) Beck. His most famous character is Captain Marvel, also known as Shazam, who lives on today. The original Captain Marvel was Billy Batson, a boy who could change himself into a grown-up superhero. Beck told Billy's story with simple but dynamic illustrations. Billy was a child, after all, and he saw the world through a child's eyes. Beck's style helped make *Captain Marvel* the most popular comic of the 1940s. His work has inspired many other comic book artists at Marvel and other comic publishing companies.

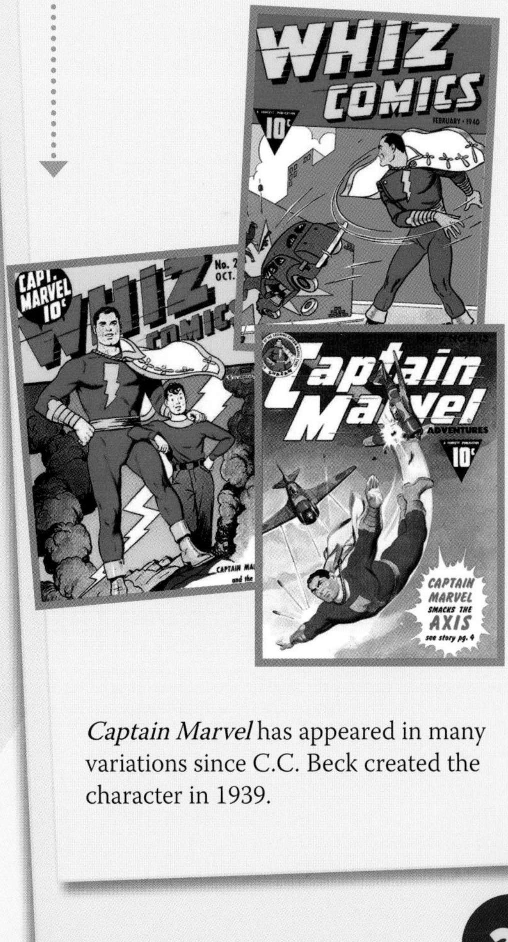
WHIZ COMICS
10¢
FEBRUARY • 1940
CAPT. MARVEL 10¢
WHIZ COMICS
Captain Marvel
ADVENTURES
10¢
CAPTAIN MARVEL SMACKS THE AXIS
see story pg. 4

Captain Marvel has appeared in many variations since C.C. Beck created the character in 1939.

STRIKING SPLASH PAGES

When comic book artists want to go big, they use splash pages. A splash page usually has just one large panel. It can be a single page or can spread across two pages. Either way, the big picture grabs the reader's attention. Splash pages often set the scene at the start of a comic or show the grand finale. But they can turn up anywhere the artist wants to turn up the action and drama.

2

Oh, no, someone messed up our recycling overnight again!
I heard it was a ghost!
We're going to get in BIG trouble with the camp counselor for littering!
What do we do?!
We need a STAKEOUT to catch this villain!
CABIN #3
This looks like a job for SUPERSTAR!

3

OH, NO, SOMEONE MESSED UP OUR RECYCLING OVERNIGHT AGAIN!
I HEARD IT WAS A GHOST!
WE'RE GOING TO GET IN BIG TROUBLE WITH THE CAMP COUNSELOR FOR LITTERING!
WHAT DO WE DO?!
WE NEED A STAKEOUT TO CATCH THIS VILLAIN!
CABIN #3
CAMP SUPER
THIS IS A JOB FOR SUPERSTAR!

4

OH, NO, SOMEONE MESSED UP OUR RECYCLING OVERNIGHT AGAIN!
I HEARD IT WAS A GHOST!
WE'RE GOING TO GET IN BIG TROUBLE WITH THE CAMP COUNSELOR FOR LITTERING!
WHAT DO WE DO?!
WE NEED A STAKEOUT TO CATCH THIS VILLAIN!
CABIN #3
CAMP SUPER
THIS IS A JOB FOR SUPERSTAR!

PROJECT GUIDES

1. Choose an idea and characters for a splash page.
2. Do a rough sketch of the page using stick figures. Then put in the word balloons.
3. Check the sketch and make changes if needed. Go over it with clean lines. Erase the guidelines.
4. Color your drawing.

Tip

You can use a partial splash page if that works best. Smaller panels can go below or even on top of part of the splash. Use them to make an important point or show a key clue!

DOC STRANGE

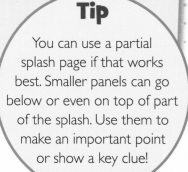

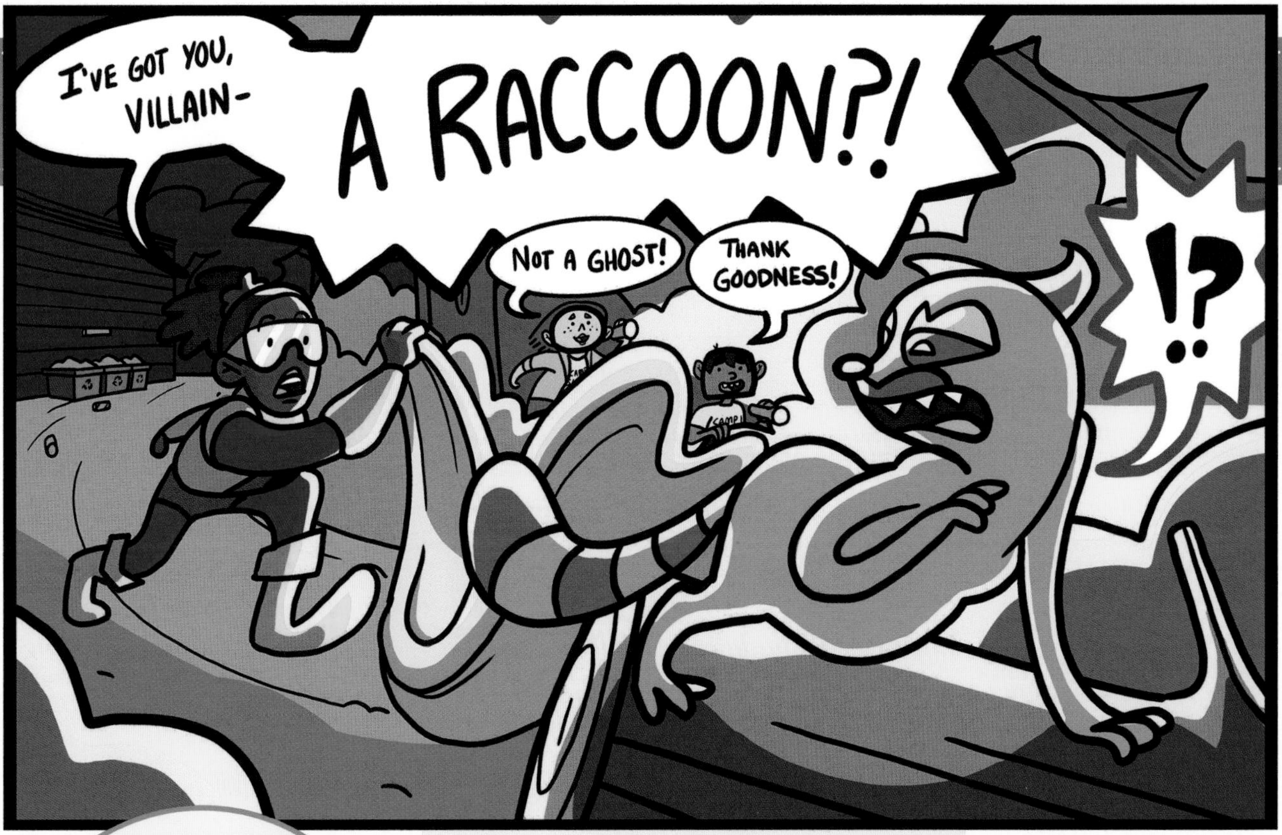
I'VE GOT YOU, VILLAIN-
A RACCOON?!
NOT A GHOST!
THANK GOODNESS!
!?

Tip

Manga artists love splash panels. Some manga start with a gorgeous splash panel that isn't even part of the story! Others are almost all splash panels with few words.

A two-page splash packs the most punch of all. The extra space allows the artist to show more details and cover more ground. Heroes look larger, villains and creatures look scarier. Some splash pages have no gutter between the two sides. Others have a gutter but the drawing goes across parts of it to connect the sides. Experiment with drawing a splash panel both ways.

WILL EISNER

(1917 – 2005) United States

New Yorker Will Eisner was a master of the splash page. He started as a comic book artist when he was still a teenager. The Golden Age of Comics was beginning and there was a lot of opportunity. Eisner liked to try newer techniques such as splash pages. In the 1940s, his superhero comic *The Spirit* was hugely popular. It appeared in 20 different Sunday newspapers, and millions of people read it every week. After the Golden Age, he began trying longer forms of comics. He is often called the father of the graphic novel. Museums and libraries host traveling shows of Eisner's artwork.

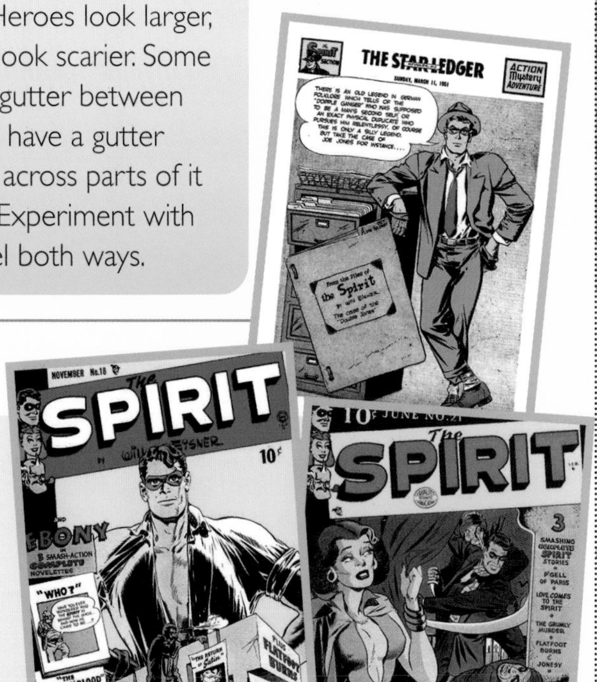
THE STAR-LEDGER
SPIRIT
SPIRIT

Will Eisner often used a splash page for both the cover and the first page of a comic, including *The Spirit*.

JUDGING A BOOK BY THE COVER?

The first chance a comic book artist has to grab a reader's attention is when they see the cover. Comics need a catchy title and great cover to give readers an idea of how exciting or funny the story will be. The cover also displays the publication date, the issue number, and the author's name. This information is important for comic collectors. Rare comics in good condition can be very valuable, if the cover is in good shape. Try drawing a cover for a superhero comic.

PROJECT GUIDES

1 Come up with a great title for your comic book. Write the title on the cover.

2 Decide what scene you want to show on the cover. The drama of an action scene will draw readers into your comic. Draw the superhero on the cover.

3 Add the super villain to the scene on the cover. Give the super villain an air of mystery and menace to build up the drama.

4 Draw other characters that will appear in your story.

5 Draw in the background, speech balloons, and other details. Make sure it's part of the story inside!

6 When you are happy with the cover, go over it with clean lines. Erase the guidelines.

7 Color your cover. Show the finished cover to your family and friends. They may have valuable ideas on how to make it even better! Always listen to what your readers have to say, because your story is for them.

1

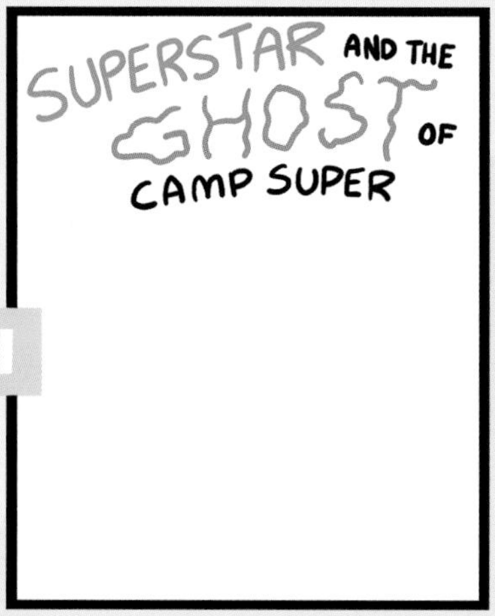
SUPERSTAR AND THE GHOST OF CAMP SUPER

2

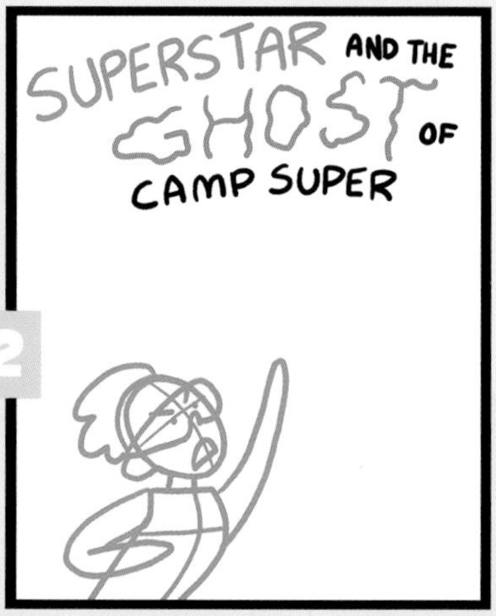
SUPERSTAR AND THE GHOST OF CAMP SUPER

3

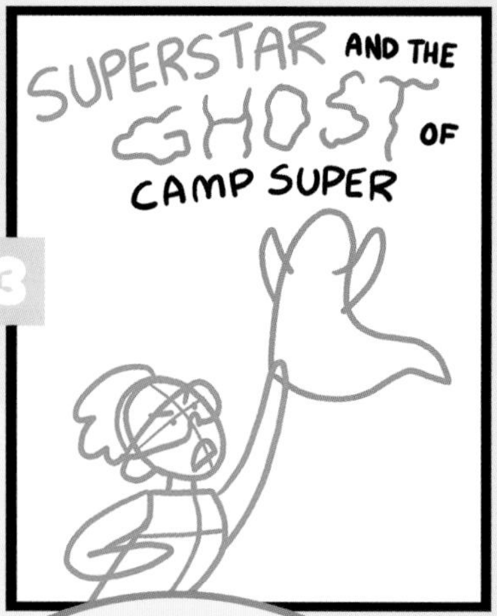
SUPERSTAR AND THE GHOST OF CAMP SUPER

4

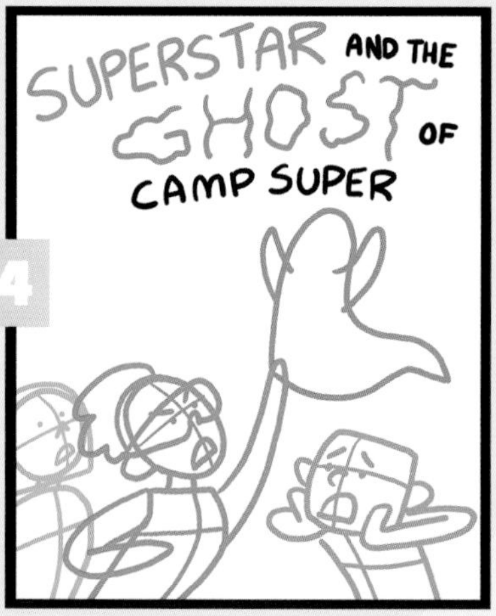
SUPERSTAR AND THE GHOST OF CAMP SUPER

5

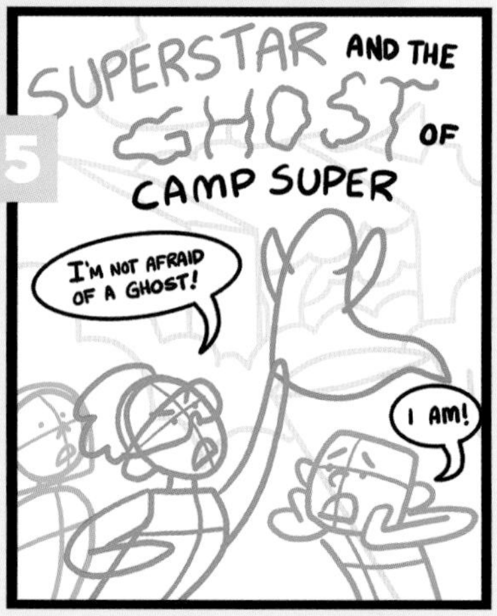
SUPERSTAR AND THE GHOST OF CAMP SUPER
I'M NOT AFRAID OF A GHOST!
I AM!

Tip

Before you create your comic book cover, go to a comic book store or look online for samples of other artists' work. The best comic book covers are great works of art! Some covers are more realistic and others are **stylized** to make them more funny or scary. After studying some great covers, decide what style you want to use for your own.

6

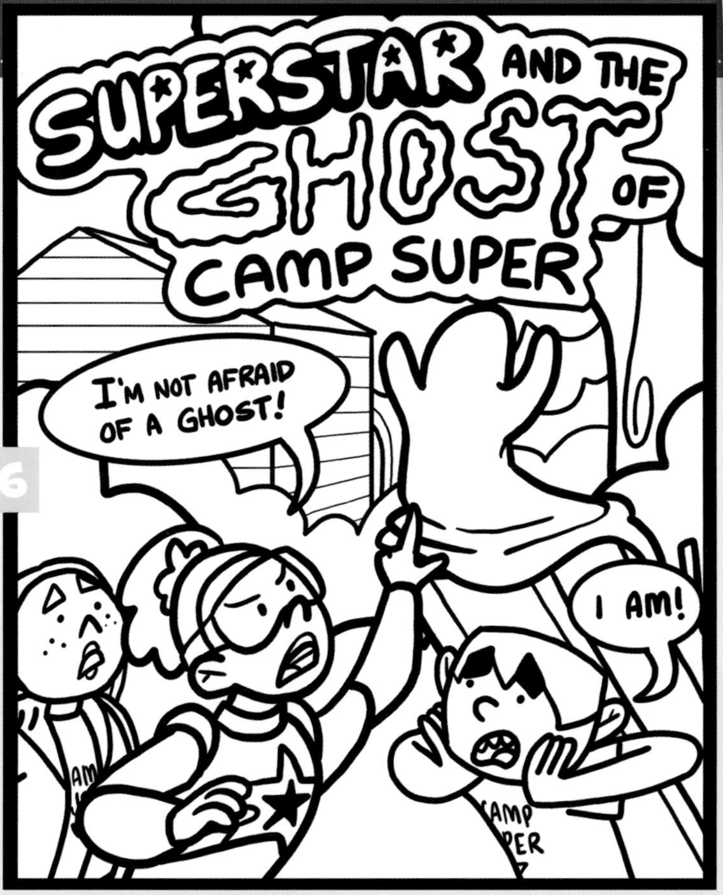
SUPERSTAR AND THE GHOST OF CAMP SUPER
I'M NOT AFRAID OF A GHOST!
I AM!
CAMP SUPER

7

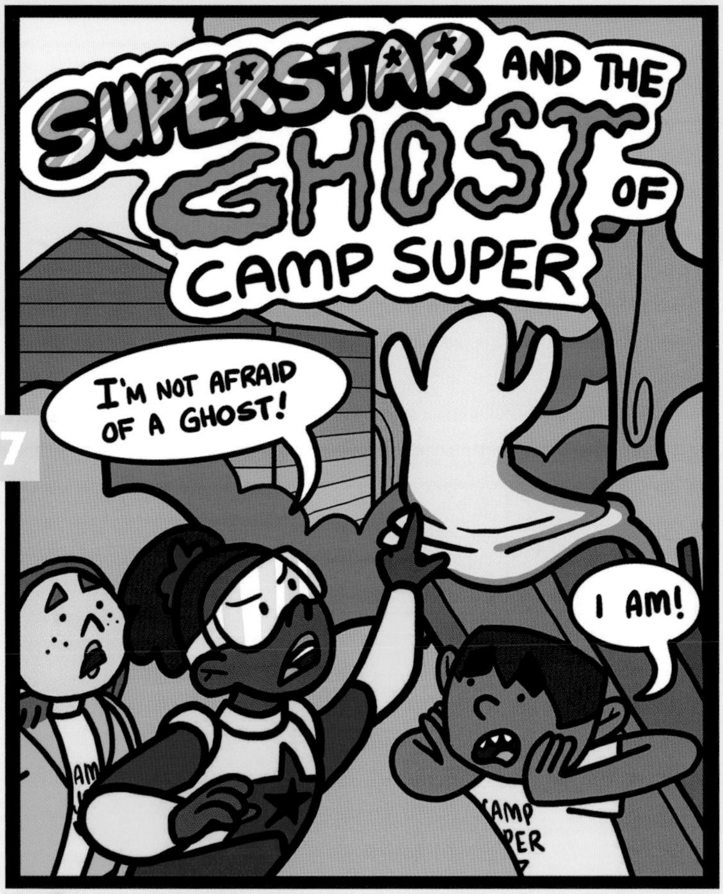
SUPERSTAR AND THE GHOST OF CAMP SUPER
I'M NOT AFRAID OF A GHOST!
I AM!
CAMP SUPER

ALEXANDER A. SCHOMBURG

(1905 – 1998) Puerto Rico

Alexander Schomburg drew more than 500 spectacular covers during the Golden Age of Comics. He was born in Puerto Rico and went to New York City in the 1920s. He and three of his brothers all became artists, Alex loved science fiction, and his work stood out because he was so good at drawing planes, rockets, and anything mechanical. He drew covers and splash pages for many different comics, including *Captain America, Green Hornet,* and *Speed.* When the Golden Age ended, he kept right on drawing for science fiction magazines.

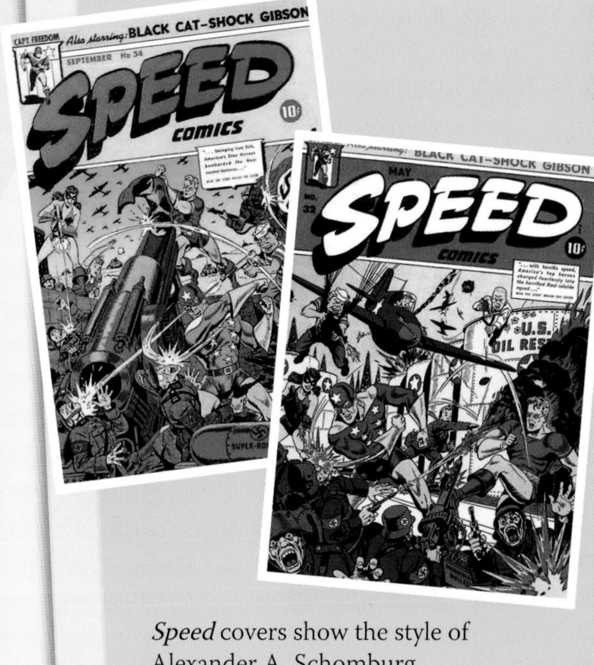
CAPT. FREEDOM
Also starring: BLACK CAT-SHOCK GIBSON
SEPTEMBER No 34
SPEED COMICS
10¢
BLACK CAT-SHOCK GIBSON
MAY
SPEED COMICS
10¢
U.S.

Speed covers show the style of Alexander A. Schomburg.

CREATE YOUR COMIC BOOK

The next step after a four-panel comic strip is creating a whole comic book. Come up with an idea for a longer story. List the characters and sketch what they will look like. Make another list of backgrounds. Outline the action and decide what will happen in each panel. Brainstorm a great title and a cover splash that will make readers want to turn the page. Figure out how many inside pages and panels you will need. When that's all done, you will be ready to draw your comic book. You don't need a lot of pages to start with. As you become more skilled, you can make longer comics.

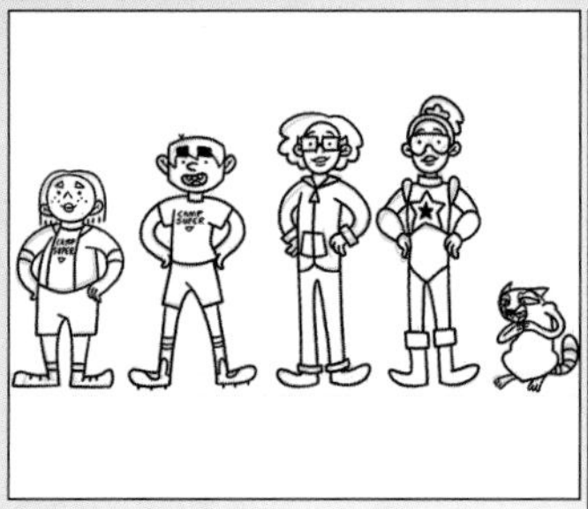

Design your characters before you start drawing your comic.

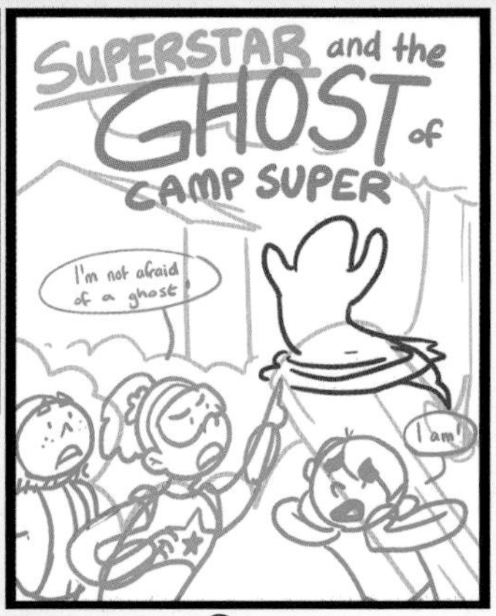
SUPERSTAR and the GHOST of CAMP SUPER
I'm not afraid of a ghost!
I am!

Cover

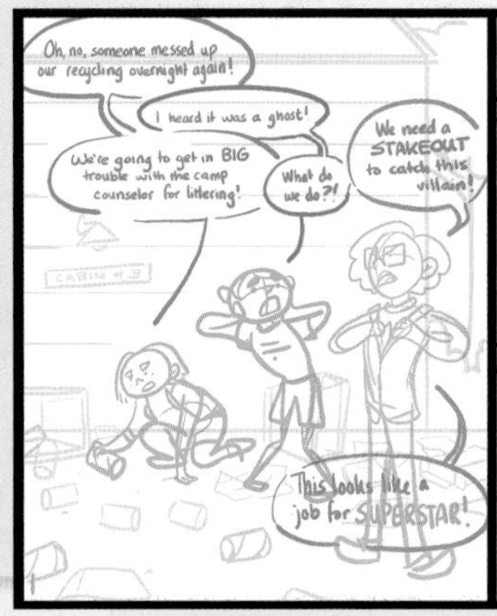
Oh, no, someone messed up our recycling overnight again!
I heard it was a ghost!
We're going to get in BIG trouble with the camp counselor for littering!
What do we do?!
We need a STAKEOUT to catch this villain!
This looks like a job for SUPERSTAR!

Splash page

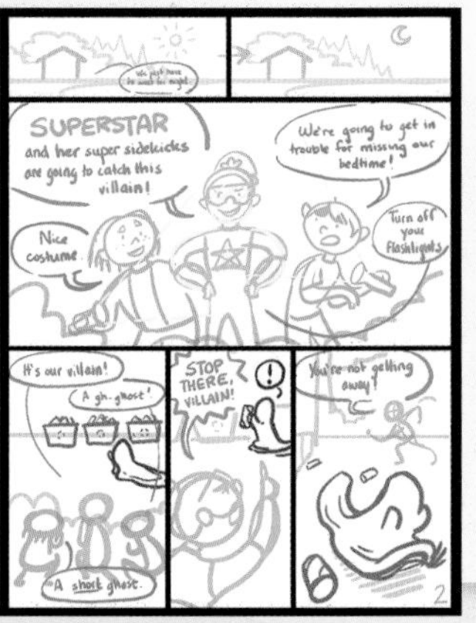
SUPERSTAR and her super sidekicks are going to catch this villain!
We're going to get in trouble for missing our bedtime!
Nice costume
Turn off your flashlights
It's our villain!
A gh.. ghost!
STOP THERE, VILLAIN!
You're not getting away!

Panels (six-panel grid)

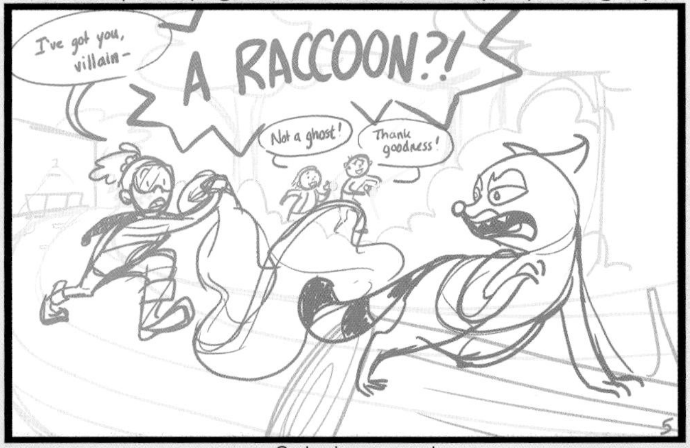
I've got you, villain-
A RACCOON?!
Not a ghost!
Thank goodness!

Splash spread

PROJECT GUIDES

- Use your outline to write a **script** for your comic. Tell what happens in every panel, including the dialogue.
- Create a general layout to match the script. How many panels will be on each page? Where will splash pages go? Vary the number, size, and shape of panels to keep readers interested.
- Draw a rough layout for each panel with simple characters. Add word balloons.
- Add details and background. At this stage, your comic should look somewhat like the sketch on the right.
- Check your work and fix problems. Draw it with clean lines. Erase the guidelines.
- Color your comic book to finish your comic art project.

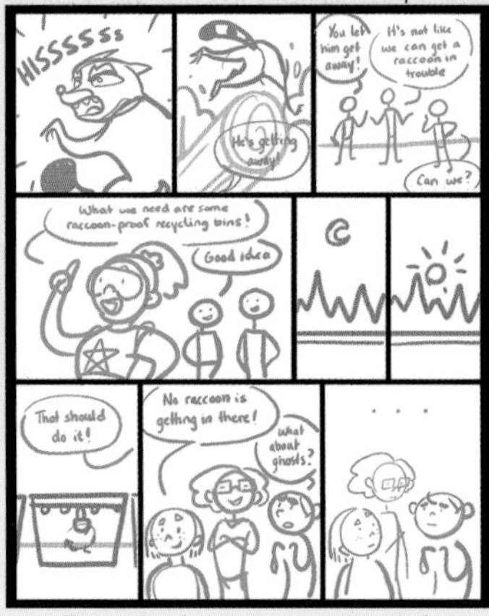
HISSSSSs
He's getting away!
You let him get away!
It's not like we can get a raccoon in trouble
Can we?
What we need are some raccoon-proof recycling bins!
Good idea
That should do it!
No raccoon is getting in there!
What about ghosts?
. . .

Panels (nine-panel grid)

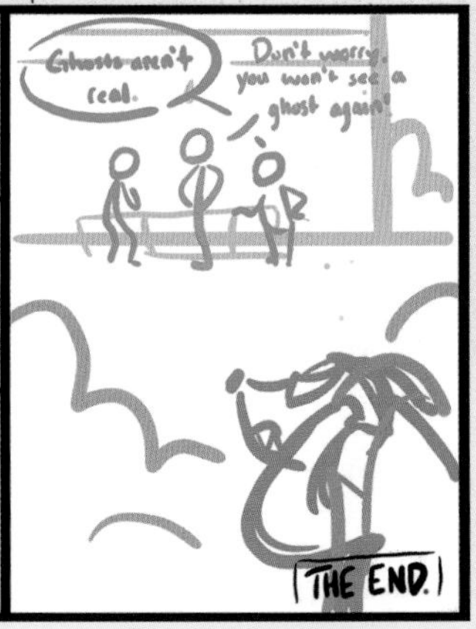
Ghosts aren't real.
Don't worry, you won't see a ghost again!
THE END

Splash page

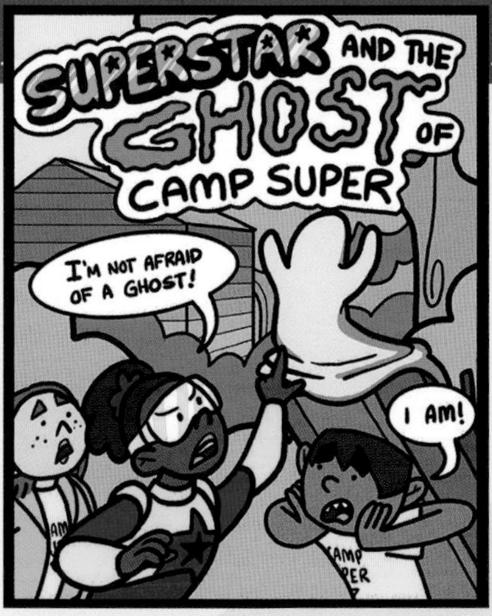
SUPERSTAR AND THE GHOST OF CAMP SUPER
I'M NOT AFRAID OF A GHOST!
I AM!

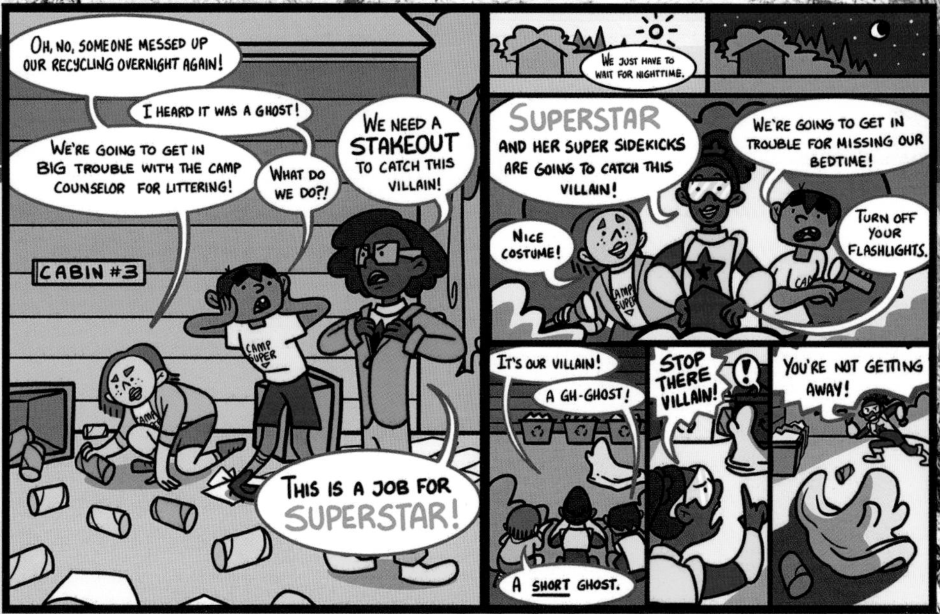
OH, NO, SOMEONE MESSED UP OUR RECYCLING OVERNIGHT AGAIN!
I HEARD IT WAS A GHOST!
WE'RE GOING TO GET IN BIG TROUBLE WITH THE CAMP COUNSELOR FOR LITTERING!
WHAT DO WE DO?!
WE NEED A STAKEOUT TO CATCH THIS VILLAIN!
CABIN #3
THIS IS A JOB FOR SUPERSTAR!
WE JUST HAVE TO WAIT FOR NIGHTTIME.
SUPERSTAR AND HER SUPER SIDEKICKS ARE GOING TO CATCH THIS VILLAIN!
WE'RE GOING TO GET IN TROUBLE FOR MISSING OUR BEDTIME!
NICE COSTUME!
TURN OFF YOUR FLASHLIGHTS.
IT'S OUR VILLAIN!
A GH-GHOST!
A SHORT GHOST.
STOP THERE VILLAIN!
!
YOU'RE NOT GETTING AWAY!

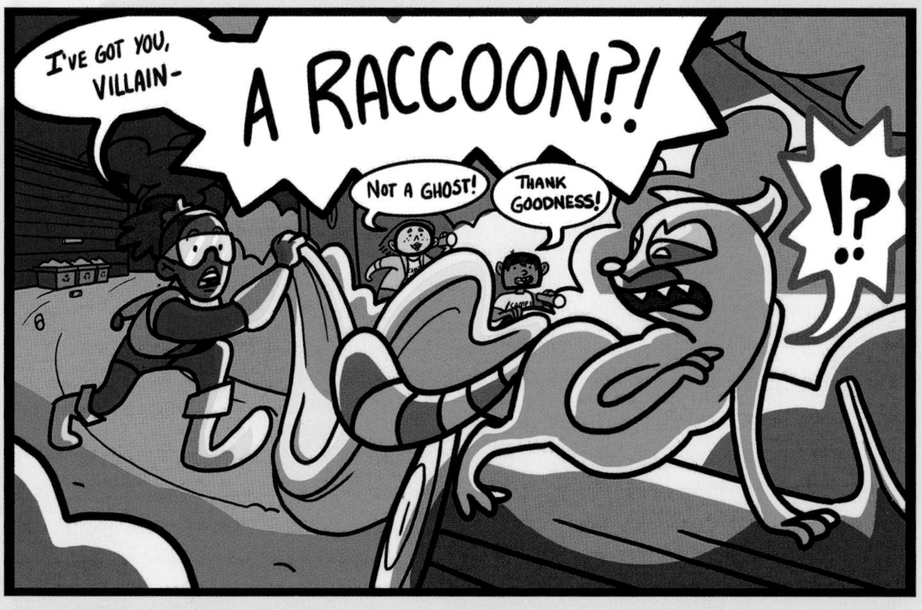
I'VE GOT YOU, VILLAIN-
A RACCOON?!
NOT A GHOST!
THANK GOODNESS!
!?

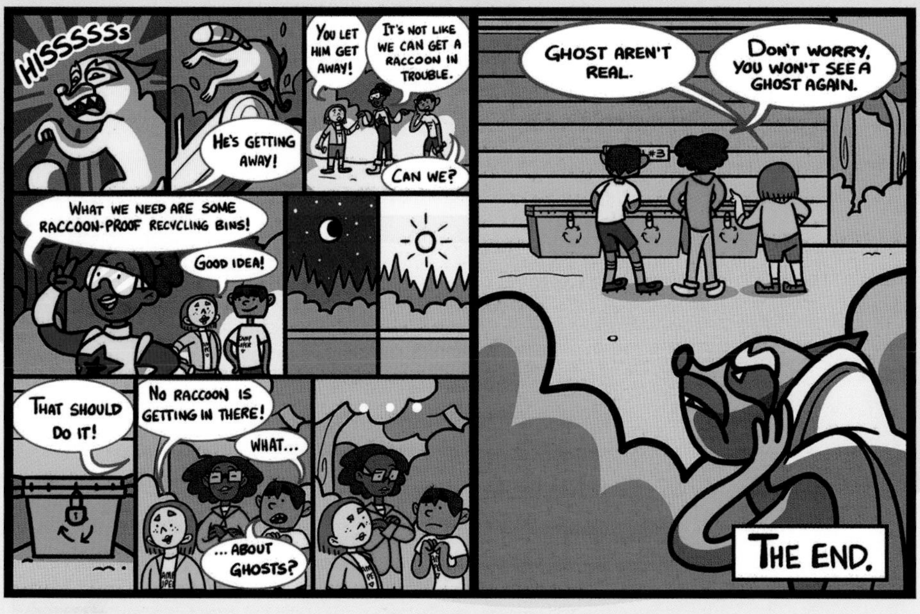
HISSSSSS
HE'S GETTING AWAY!
YOU LET HIM GET AWAY!
IT'S NOT LIKE WE CAN GET A RACCOON IN TROUBLE.
CAN WE?
WHAT WE NEED ARE SOME RACCOON-PROOF RECYCLING BINS!
GOOD IDEA!
THAT SHOULD DO IT!
NO RACCOON IS GETTING IN THERE!
WHAT...
... ABOUT GHOSTS?
GHOST AREN'T REAL.
DON'T WORRY, YOU WON'T SEE A GHOST AGAIN.
THE END.

MAKE A COMIC BOOK!

If you feel like you have mastered the basics of creating a comic book layout and storytelling, you are ready to make a comic book! Follow the steps below to create an eight-page comic book that you can carry around with you to show your family and friends.

1. Stack two sheets of paper and fold lengthwise. Crease the fold. This will give you an eight-page comic. (You can have more or fewer pages, but not so many that the book gets too difficult to handle.)
2. Number each page at the bottom from 1 to 8. Separate the pages.
3. Draw your cover on page 1.
4. Plan a layout that will carry your story through pages 2 to 8. Page 8 is the last page. It could be another splash page to give your comic book a striking finish.
5. Draw the story. Remember to go from page 2 to page 3 and so on.
6. Put the book back together. Use the page numbers to get them in the right order.
7. Staple two or three times along the fold.

IS MANGA YOUR STYLE?

Manga is a style of comic book that is wildly popular in Japan, where it started, and all over the world. When manga comics are turned into animated movies, they are called anime. Manga characters usually have big eyes and weird hair, but they tend to be more realistic than many other styles of cartoon. Their emotions, though, are exaggerated. They cry buckets of tears when they are sad and emit steam when they are angry! Like all comics, manga can have many themes. Some are action-packed while others tell a love story. Think of Pokemon and Dragon Ball Z—they're manga! Now, try your hand at manga style.

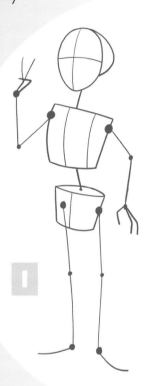

1

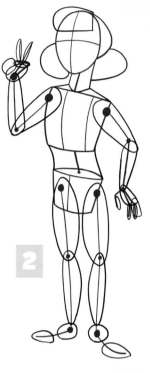

2

PROJECT GUIDES

1. Draw an egg shape for a head. Use a square for the top of the torso and a trapezoid for the bottom. Use lines to connect the torso parts and make arms and legs.

2. Use the skeleton technique from page 9 to fill out the figure.

3. Turn the skeleton figure into a more realistic outline of your character. Go over the drawing with a thicker pencil. Add more details like hair.

4. Erase any guidelines that have not become part of your character. Add final details and color.

3

4

MANGA STYLE EYES

Manga eyes are huge, round, and full of expression.

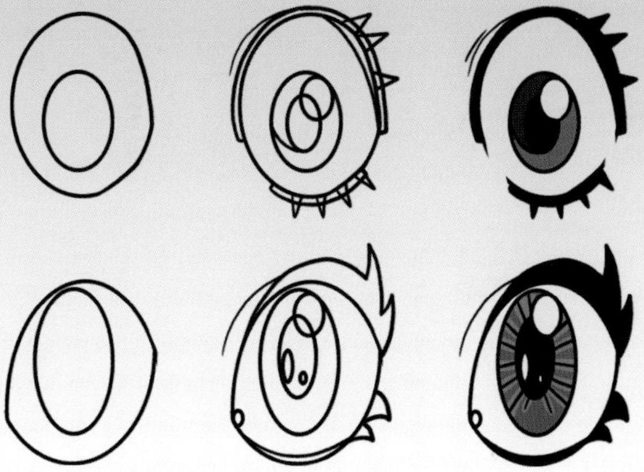

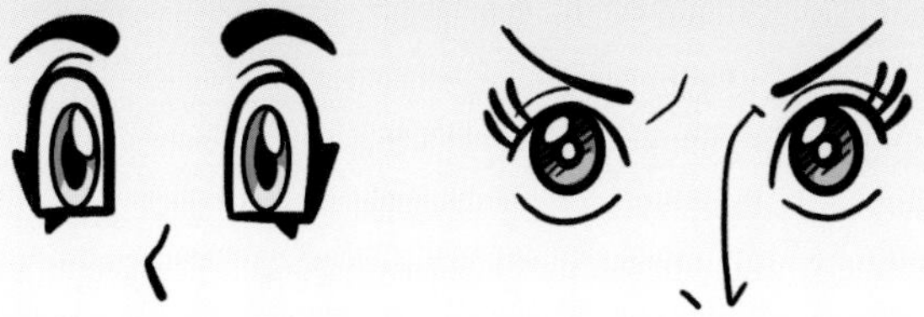

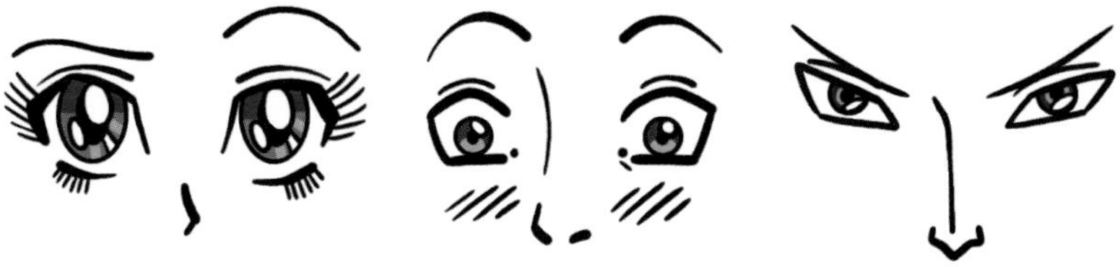

Did You Know?

Manga means "humorous drawing" in Japanese. Manga got its start in the 1100s and 1200s. Like comics worldwide, today's manga can be serious or silly, and manga artists use many different styles.

MANGA STYLE HAIR

Manga hair is wild, thick, and bright. It's easier to draw than to get the same look in real life!

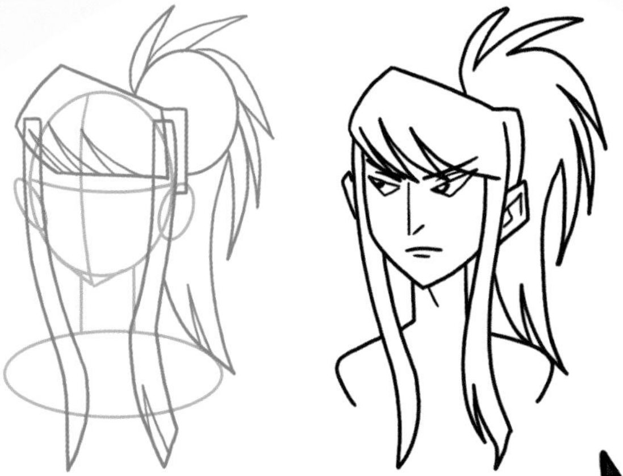

Outline the basic shape of a hairdo before drawing individual strands.

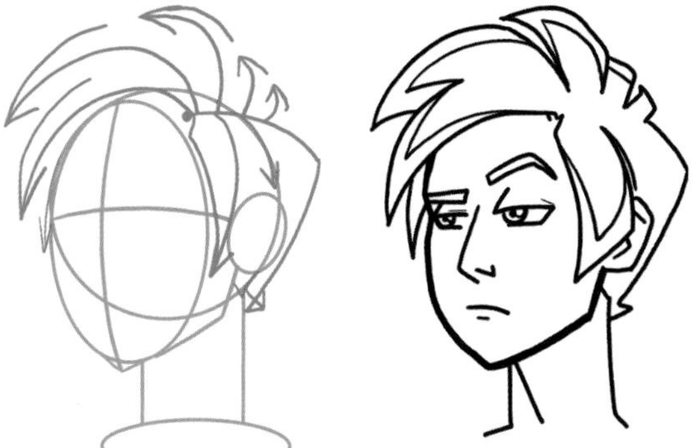

Hair looks most natural when it all **radiates** from the top of the head. You can change this for special effects.

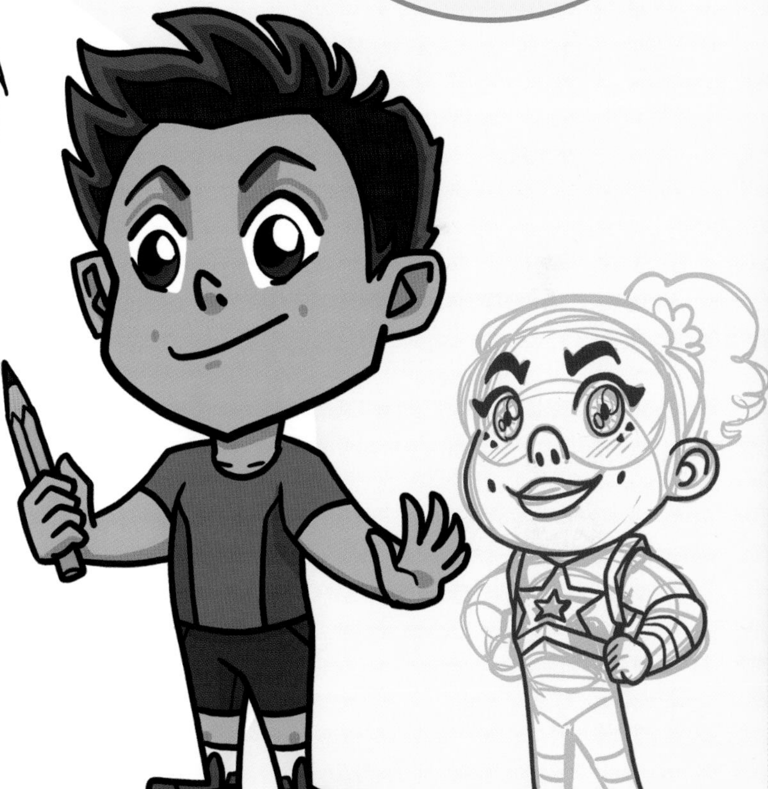

Looking sharp comes naturally to manga characters, because they are drawn with sharp angles and spiky hair.

LEARNING MORE

BOOKS

Finnegan, Marco. *Garfield's Guide to Creating Your Own Comic Strip.*
Lerner Publications, 2019.

Roche, Art. *Art for Kids: Cartooning: The Only Cartooning Book You'll Ever Need to Be the Artist You've Always Wanted to Be.* Sterling Publishers, 2010.

Sautter, Aaron. *How to Draw Batman, Superman, and Other DC Super Heroes and Villains.* Capstone Young Readers, 2015.

Wadsworth, Ginger. *Born to Draw Comics: The Story of Charles Schulz and the Creation of Peanuts.* Henry Holt and Co., 2019.

WEBSITES

Pixton Comics

www.pixton.com

An interactive website featuring Click-n-Drag Comics to create your own comics. There are also video tutorials to learn all about making comics.

Make Beliefs Comix

www.makebeliefscomix.com/

A great introduction to comics. You can create comics online or choose from a large selection of printables that will help you get started drawing and writing your own comics.

Drawing for Kids

www.artforkidshub.com/how-to-draw/

This website features a large collection of videos on how to draw—anything!

Drawing Tutorials

www.hellokids.com/r_12/drawing-for-kids

This website features a great collection of drawing tutorials.

GLOSSARY

allegory A story that teaches a lesson, often using animal characters

clean lines Smooth, crisp lines and borders that stand out from a background

dialogue The exact words of a conversation between two or more speakers

economic Relating to the making, selling, and using of goods or services

exaggerate To describe something as larger or greater than it really is

genre A category or type of book or art, such as a Western or science fiction

Golden Age of Comics A period of time, or era, in the production of American comic books when many of the most iconic characters and books were created

horizon line Where the ground meets the sky

italics A style of lettering that slants

layout The design or arrangement of something

manga A Japanese style of comic books and graphic novels

motivation The reason behind a person or character's action

narration Spoken or written words that tell what is happening in a creative work

radiate To spread out from a central point

quirk An odd or unusual habit or behavior

script The complete written text of a creative work, including narration, dialogue, and descriptions of action

stylized Created according to an artistic pattern rather than nature

techniques The ways in which things are done to accomplish a goal

theme The subject or important idea of a work of art, music, or writing

torso Central part of the human body, not including the head, arms, and legs

two-dimensional Having height and width but not depth. If all three are present, the scene or object is 3-D (three-dimensional)

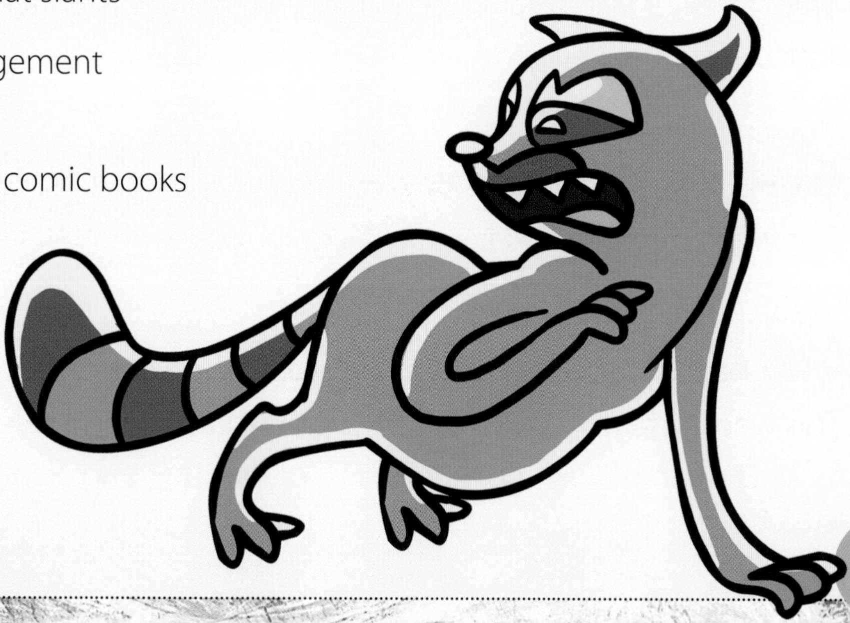

INDEX

ABOUT THE AUTHOR

Jane Yates studied art at the OCAD and Ryerson University. She worked as a freelance photographer before shifting to children's publishing where she's worked as a designer, writer, editor and creative director. Combining her vast experience in children's book publishing and her love for arts and crafts, Yates has authored over twenty craft books for children and makes her home with her family, two giant dogs, and an attack cat.